THE LITTLE VICTIMS PLAY
An Edwardian Childhood

This book is due for return on or before the last date shown above; it may, subject to the book not being reserved by another reader, be renewed by personal application, post, or telephone, quoting this date and details of the book.

100% recycled paper.

HAMPSHIRE COUNTY COUNCIL
County Library

THE LITTLE VICTIMS PLAY

An Edwardian Childhood

by

VERA RYDER

ROBERT HALE · LONDON

© Vera Ryder 1974
First published in Great Britain 1974

ISBN 0 7091 4646 9

Composed by Specialised Offset Services Ltd
and printed in Great Britain by
Lowe & Brydone Ltd
Thetford, Norfolk

3710

To the memory of my parents
with affection, admiration and gratitude

Alas, regardless of their doom
The little victims play!
No sense have they of ills to come,
Nor care beyond today.

Yet ah! why should they know their fate?
Since sorrow never comes too late,
And happiness too swiftly flies.
Thought would destroy their paradise.
No more; where ignorance is bliss,
'Tis folly to be wise.

Thomas Gray

Contents

Illustrations

I

Earliest Memories

A pale Chinese carpet with a border of pink roses covered the drawing-room floor. I remember it clearly, for nearly every evening of my crawling days were spent with nose and eyes a few centimetres above it scuttling in panic haste over its soft warm surface. In panic haste indeed I crawl but filled with delicious excitement because my father crawls behind me, roaring like a lion. We dive under a bridge of cushions balanced from the end of the sofa to a chair; he catches me up onto his shoulder and carries me over to the fireplace where, on the shelf above lies my mother's collection of old silver crucifixes and trinkets. I gaze at these, fascinated as always by their shining beauty, and as always am allowed to hold in my hot little hands the cold silver fish with red eyes and waggly tail. This is a delightful piece of work, the jointed scales making the movements astonishingly life-like. So realistically does its tail waggle that the thought never enters my head that it is not a real fish. That is has no water to swim in does not worry me, it seems happy enough lying on the yellow marble shelf among the other shining things. So I put it back between the crucifix and the little vinaigrette and go upstairs with my nannie who has come to fetch me to bed.

I have another vivid memory of about the same time and this is when my great-grandfather, Sir Francis Cook, the first baronet, died. Up till then I had been the lucky possessor of two great-grandfathers (my mother's grandfather, the first Viscount Bridport being the other), two grandfathers and two grandmothers. Sir Francis died on 17th February 1901, two days after my second birthday and a month later than Queen Victoria. Because of the following trivial happening the day of the funeral has been indelibly fixed in my memory.

I stand on a chair in my Father's dressing room, so that I may more easily see myself in the mirror on the wall, and beside me stands my small, rosy-cheeked nannie White ready to catch me should i fall. The door opens and into the room flock a mass of people headed of course by my parents, all in deepest black like a colony of rooks. They crowd round me exclaiming at my angelic appearance, for I, alone, am clad in white from top to toe. I feel like a prima donna taking a call. This small personal success at such a tender age has blotted out all other events of the day.

It is, of course, possible that I am wrong in attributing this scene to the day of my great-grandfather's funeral; it could just as easily have happened when the old Queen died. The fact that I was all in white and surrounded by the mourning rooks does not mean it must have been a *family* death. The whole Empire mourned the Queen as head of an enormous family; she was a personal loss to all its members and everyone who could afford to donned deepest black. In this instance there was only a month's difference in the dates and I was sublimely unconscious of any loss, either way.

In these short sketches I make no attempt to write a chronological account of my childhood, perhaps not even an entirely accurate one. After all, who could possibly be interested in the daily happenings in the life of a small child growing up in the orderly discipline of a late Victorian-Edwardian family? Seen from a distance as I am now doing, much is indistinct like a fading photograph, but 'distance lends enchantment' and therefore with many of the less enjoyable details blurred or conveniently forgotten the happier events seem more brilliant in comparison. The trouble is that I hardly know where to begin when so many of these snapshots of the past come tumbling out of the memory album. So many would appear to be such small insignificant happenings that one wonders why they should have remained bright and clear while more momentous events have been forgotten. A child's world is very small so that everything tends to assume vast proportions and therefore leaves strong impressions. For instance, what could be more trivial than the following most vividly remembered scene?

I was staying at Bognor with my maternal grandparents, the Bridports, and could not have been more than three years old. On this occasion Nannie White and I were out walking – toddling might be more accurate – when we found ourselves in a field which boasted a rubbish heap in one corner. From the pile of rusty pots and pans I selected an old kettle which I proceeded to kick around. To my enormous delight Nannie joined in the game and oh, the din that poor old kettle made as we walloped it about. For me, its cracked tinny protesting voice was music of unearthly charm!

Thinking about the kettle and that exhilarating experience I realise that I have more early memories of Sudley Lodge, Bognor and its occupants than of my own home at Esher. I certainly remember more details about the nursery routine and daily events there. I suppose this is because I had a more exciting life at Bognor, for I was the first grand-child and Grannie did everything she could for my happiness. I expect the discipline was also less oppressive. I was not a spoilt child; far from it, so I suppose the slightly less strait-laced routine was more welcome. In other words. Grannie (as Grannies usually do) spoilt me! And of course staying at Sudley Lodge did not happen often enough to take the shine out of the event, so that every day seemed to be better and more exciting than the one before. Here is another strong unfaded snap-shot still ridiculously clear and of no importance whatever.

Soon after I was three I ceased to be the only pebble on the beach when a distant relative of my father, a girl eighteen months older than myself came to live with us and share my life. Olga Balfour was the third of the four daughters of James and Maud Balfour and I suppose the rather impoverished parents were glad that one of their girls at least would have an assured education and upbringing in the rich relation's family. At our tender ages of three and four the plots and plans of the grown-ups meant nothing to us; we could barely see beyond the end of our noses anyhow. Thus the absurd picture emerges of our first meeting, which to both of us to this day remains as clear as though it had happened only yesterday; not because either of us was greatly attracted to each other or even loathed each other on sight. No, the one thing we remember about that first meeting was the fact that we both wore brown kid gloves. But that was not all; something else made an even greater impression on our little minds. As we were driving home in the brougham from Oxshott station, Olga sitting on Nannie's lap, I on Mother's, we barely glanced at one another and certainly never uttered a word because we were staring intently at our gloved hands spread out upon our knees. To my surprise and growing indignation I saw that, unlike my own plain stitched ones, Olga's gloves had black lines down the back of each finger! In different circumstances I wonder what might not have been the outcome of such provocation? In fact, I said nothing, but from thence forward I regarded Olga with respect, acknowledging her superiority in glove style as well as in age.

I had just had my fourth birthday when my sister Rachel was born, and as soon as possible Nannie took Olga and me up to London to see her. Rachel was born at 24 Hyde Park Gardens, the Cook's London house, one of those tall white Victorian residences with a vast, cold, dark hall with a black and white chequered floor from which rose a fine white winding staircase to the circular gallery round the first landing. Here was mother's room and we went in wondering what we were going to see. We knew, of course, there was a new baby but there had been nothing to prepare my mind for the sight that met my astonished eyes. There was mother lying in bed; my heart gave a bound — was she ill? She was smiling happily at us and pointing to a fantastic creation of spotted muslin, lace and satin bows standing near by. I cannot remember the baby at all, only my mother half-smothered in billowing sheets and satin eiderdown, her lovely red hair spread over the lace-edged pillows and the fragrance of the flower filled room.

2
Mother and Home Life

Our childhood was spent almost entirely at home except for visits to our maternal grandparents at Bognor and to some seaside resort every summer for the good of our health. The present custom of dragging children around on the Continent or further afield was not considered desirable and anyhow quite unnecessary in those days of nannies and governesses; but in fact our parents did very little travelling themselves. I suppose there was not the same urge to get away from it all — what was there to get away from anyhow? We could still move about our own lovely countryside in comfort, for there were few motor-cars on the roads and no mile upon mile of frustrated, neurotic, jammed-up travellers patiently or impatiently struggling to get from A to Z. In our case, as in many others in our position, our home was a place to live in all the year round except for our yearly seaside trips. I never put my nose out of England till I was thirteen when we went to Cintra in Portugal for the Easter holidays. I am sure we would never even have gone there had it not been that grandpapa Cook was the lucky inheritor of that wondrous fairyland called Monserrate, which was always shouting loudly to the family and their friends to come and enjoy its beauty. In my opinion, I think a certain amount of foreign travel contributes towards a more mature personality apart from the obvious enjoyment it brings. In my case, I had to wait till my brother, nine years my junior, was considered old enough to make the perilous journey; it never seemed to have struck my parents that even if Francis was too young, I certainly was not.

My very first home was at Weybridge, a comparatively easy train journey to London for my father who went to the City every day. Maybe he found Weybridge unnecessarily far out, for when I was two we moved to Esher, a little nearer to London. I remember nothing about the Weybridge house; all my memories are entwined around Copseham where we lived for eighteen years until we moved to Doughty House, Richmond, after Grandpapa Cook's death.

Copseham stood on the then quiet country road between Esher and Oxshott. A green stretch of common land and a little round sandy hill lay along one side of the garden; beyond were the woods, mostly pines and birch, and, in the open, stretches of heather and gorse and bracken. It was rather boggy and soggy through the woods and in the middle lay a sinister pond called the Black Pool which I never liked since the day the body of some poor woman had been dragged out of it. In the winter it sometimes froze over so hard that it was soon covered with shouting, skating figures flying hither and thither, greatly enjoying themselves. But I never could forget that poor drowned woman and hated the place.

No other house was in sight in those early days and the traffic consisted mainly of tradesmen's carts and our own carriages. Copseham had no architectural distinction, its only claim to fame seems to have been that once George Meredith had lived there. Soon it began to grow as the family increased and by the time we had moved to Richmond in 1919 Copseham had become what the agents would call 'a house of character', a real 'family house'.

A new nursery wing had been added with schoolroom, pantry and servants' hall. The old dining-room and the drawing-room with the pale Chinese carpet had been made into one big dining-room. Finally, a music room, designed by the architect Guy Dawber, was built at right angles to the drawing-room and gave an imposing and delightful finish to the place. The zig-zag oak stairway, which looked as if it had sprung from the big clump of rhododendrons near by and which climbed up the end of the house ending in the billiard room, remained where it was and became an indoor staircase, the music-room growing up round it.

The music-room was a good room for sound with its high vaulted plaster ceiling and it was the focal point of all our activities, both solemn and frivolous. Mother had no use for a drawing-room as such, it would have cramped her style. For Mother, despite her diminutive frame had big ideas; there was nothing miniature about her inspirations. She needed a place in which to entertain her friends with no restrictions and no cluttering up with the usual drawing-room knick-knacks. Her collection of silver crucifixes and, of course, the silver fish were still lying on the yellow marble shelf over the fire-place in the (now) big dining-room. The music-room would have scorned being referred to as the drawing-room; it was the living-room with emphasis on music. In fact, the living or music-room, to me meant only that; the centre of the musical life of the house. For this we needed a piano, in our case a very lovely Steinway grand on which father and mother and, in due time, myself performed with varying degrees of success. Father, of course, had his linen-fold oak-panelled library to retire to and ourselves the nursery and later, the schoolroom. As well as being the setting for the Christmas entertainment, written and produced by mother every year, other equally important events took place in the music-room.

Morning prayers were the first item on the daily pro- gramme. The stable clock would strike eight in its peremp- tory, tinny voice. On the last stroke father pressed the bell twice to announce that he was ready and waiting. The double oak doors were flung open almost instantaneously by the butler to admit the stiff and starched procession which proceeded to march the length of the room. It was headed by the dignified and usually very robust figure of the cook, followed by housemaids, kitchen and scullery-maids with the underfootman or page-boy bringing up the rear. The butler would then close the doors quietly and join the procession moving decorously towards the rows of chairs ready waiting.

If all had gone according to plan, we children would have already been in our places beside our parents watching and waiting. But sometimes we might have left our usual scramble to get dressed just too late to reach the music-room before the staff came in; sometimes, only just in time to hear the doors closing behind it and sometimes, but only very, very occasionally, just as everybody was kneeling down and the prayers beginning. This latter was a disaster. We did our valiant best to beat the bell by rushing through the billiard room to the little door from which the staircase descended into the music-room and from where we could hear father's voice droning away below. If the door was open a crack we could catch a glimpse of him standing or kneeling by the long refrectory table, rows of bottoms opposite him; black ones, resting on the large black boots of the butler and footman, crackly pink chintz ones of the maids and the large white one of the cook.

If things had reached this stage we were too frightened even to try to creep down for father was facing the staircase down which we would have had to descend and could not have failed to see us. No, there was nothing we could do except face the paternal wrath at the breakfast table. I can assure you that we were very, very seldom late.

The other form of entertainment held in the music-room was different and more exciting than morning prayers, though not without moments of delicious anguish to the performers. This was the operetta given before household and friends every Christmas Eve. We took it for granted that mother would be writing something for us to sing and act every Christmas, and indeed I can remember only two occasions when she did not. Once, when we had a huge bran tub and mother, dressed as a chef, stirring the contents vigorously with a big wooden spoon and we, as smaller chefs, handing round branny parcels to everyone. And once when mother dressed up as Father Christmas and strode down the long grass path through the garden with a bulging sack (straw-filled, I suppose) slung over her back.

We watched her from the nursery window, a small figure in red cloak and hood, black boots, white wig and long white beard. Very blue eyes, curiously like mother's, twinkled beneath bushy white brows. It never occurred to me to suspect she (or he) was not what he (or she) appeared to be. I can only remember my almost unbearable thrill on seeing, not a story-book Father Christmas, but the real flesh and blood one walking through our garden. So excited was I standing there with nose flattened against the window pane that I was not surprised when my father, who had his arms around me, said to Olga's pretty mother, who was watching with us, 'Just feel this child's heart, Maud, she must be on the verge of a heart attack.'

Except for these two incidents the yearly Christmas show was the Operetta, written by mother, words and music. How gifted she was; poetry and music were second nature to her. She sometimes wrote to her friends letters in verse, not perhaps of the highest quality, but with the greatest facility and sense of humour. We, in our tender years, naturally could not assess the quality of either her words or her music; we took it all for granted but I know she had many friends able to appreciate these great gifts which grew and strengthened as she matured. It is a thousand pities that much of her music was never written out and that what she managed to write herself was in rather poor manuscript. Father, who was a good musician and a better pianist than she, was given the unenviable job of playing the accompaniments to these operettas from the almost indecipherable score. Only one of these operettas was published (by Novello) and this, I think, was one of the last and the best. I still have some of her manuscripts of earlier efforts and can remember some of the music and the words of others. These shows were quite elaborately put on, mother of course being the producer.

A stage was built across one end of the music-room with proper scenery and lighting and our dresses were well-made, not in the least safety-pin affairs. We must have been very young when *The Christmas Messengers* was produced because only mother, Rachel and I took part. What had happened to Olga? If I remember rightly, the poor, unfortunate Olga had not a good ear for music; she persisted in singing flat, she couldn't help it. So I suppose mother wrote only for us three.

> 'I am the Blizzard of the North,
> And sweeping through the sky
> Full-armed with spear of bitter hail,
> In cloak of grey and suit of mail
> I swoop! I whirl! I fly!'

sang mother, striding manfully towards the footlights, her small figure robed in a tattered grey frock, a dark grey cloak swirling round her shoulders, breastplate flashing, her mane of red hair topped by a winged silver helmet. With one hand she held her shield, with the other she shook her silver spear so that the sewn-on icicles tinkled freezingly. She was splendidly dramatic.

I was feeling exactly like the pale, cold jailer I was supposed to be representing, petrified with fright and the fear of not coming up to mother's expectations.

> 'I am the cool and crystal Ice,
> The Jailer of the streams,
> And still and cold and strong am I,
> Yet from my captives not a sigh,
> They sleep with silent dreams.'

I sang this, in a small thin voice, almost inaudibly. I was trembling so much that all my glass icicles covering my pale green dress clattered together and I felt anything but still and strong, just very cold. My sister must have looked enchanting as 'Snow of the Mountains' dressed all in white with cotton-wool bobbles everywhere. Although only about four she coped with her little song with great composure and brought the house down.

'Snow of the Mountains' is my name
And silently I creep,
Weaving a mantle pure and white
And whispering downwards through the night,
I send the world to sleep'.

Another very early effort was called *The Christmas Ship*. A large wooden ship with masts and sails was built on the stage. In it we sat, a crew of little female sailors — sailor suits, straw hats, lanyards and whistles. I think Olga was included in this because you see, in the chorus a little flatness was not noticeable. I think my young brother, Francis, was also there because young as he was, he stole most of the thunder from the rest of the cast having a lovely treble and a faultless ear. Mother, of course, was justifiably proud of having a young Caruso in the family. I can't remember any of us being quite so delighted. Our ship was laden with presents for everybody and as we sailed over the stage (I suppose hidden hands pulled us across) shading our eyes from the glare of the lights with most professional salutes, we burst into the opening chorus of which, stupidly, I can remember only two lines:

'Fair ship, dear ship homeward sailing,
Treasure bringing from afar . . .'

A simple, childish production but then, of course, we were very young and mother had to cut her coat to the rather skimpy amount of cloth. As we grew older and our musical talents blossomed so did mother's inventiveness, culminating in a cantata called the *Seasons*. This was quite a lengthy affair needing hours of practice. What anguish we endured, sometimes tearfully, while being put through our paces, for mother was a demanding teacher; she knew exactly what she wanted, for after all was she not author, composer and director? I think poor father suffered the most as, with pince-nez on nose he tried his best to keep up with mother's energetic tempo in the introduction to 'Winter'.

'Go on, Herbert', she cried, as she stood behind him banging out the rhythm on his shoulders as he faltered through the complicated opening bars, 'faster, faster, you *must* get the spirit of the thing'. Poor father; it was difficult enough to play, even had he been able to read the stuff, but mother's manuscript was hardly helpful. One of the choruses in 'Autumn' went as follows:

'Sleep, O Mother Earth and rest thee
Till the sun's warm kiss
Shall unfold thy snowy mantle
And restore our bliss.'

We had the greatest difficulty keeping from giggling as we sang 'restore our bliss'; we dared not even glance at each other. Why? Because we had a butler at that time called 'Bliss' and he had just given notice. We thought it terribly funny.

The household staff, the coachman and the gardener with their families came to these shows. There were also our parents' friends, one of whom, an American called Chester Fentress, became one of Mother's adoring slaves. He had a fine tenor voice and greatly to our joy was roped in on more than one occasion to help with the show. I remember him so well, a blond giant dressed as a Teddy Bear among us, the other toys, singing the following carol:

Solo: A little tiny Child upon this world once smiled.
Chorus: Jesus, our dearest, dearest Lord.
Solo: A lesson He has taught, a gift to man has brought.
Chorus: Jesus, our dearest Lord.
Solo: He taught us how to live. He showed us how to give.
Chorus: Jesus, our dearest, dearest Lord.
Solo: And so on Christmas Day we think of Him and say
Chorus: Jesus, our dearest Lord.

There were two other verses, but these two show how much Christmas meant to us and especially to mother. In spite of the excitement of tree, stockings, presents and operettas, we never forgot the reason for this Festival. Mother was profoundly religious and was deeply moved by the Christmas story so that in one way or another she always brought into our revelry reverence and gratitude for that first Christmas Day.

3

More Home Life

◆━━━◆

Mother was a clever and enthusiastic gardener. She had green
fingers, figuratively speaking, for of course all, or nearly all,
the physical work was done by William Card and his
underlings. It was mother who designed the long grass path
(really a misnomer; it should have been a 'walk') which ran
the full length of the garden from the dining-room window to
the little wrought-iron gate which led into the wood. Along
both sides of the walk, which was intersected at intervals by
three gravel paths, blazed the herbaceous border, a fine sight
in summer and a tremendous labour to maintain at such a
pitch of perfection. But labour was easy to find in those days
and the garden was a picture of colour and loveliness under
the watchful and inspired direction of mother and Card. To
get the full effect of this simple design you would have to
stand in the dining-room by the fireplace, above which was
the shelf on which mother's crucifixes and the silver fish lay,
and look out of the big window which filled the space
between the two chimney flues. The eye could thus travel
unimpeded along the full stretch of green carpet to the little
iron gate and the dark pines beyond, a matter of some 350
yards. On brick piers either side of this gate sat vindictive
looking stone eagles. Under the plank over the ditch on the
other side grew the most luxuriant crop of nettles imaginable
and the sight of us wobbling across with our wheelbarrows,
filled not only with weeds but with trusting small human
cargo inevitably destined for the nettle-bed, was watched

with malice by those hateful birds. You could distinctly hear their squawks of delight as with outstretched wings and open beaks they crouched upon their pedestals.

The rest of the garden was more usual but charming and always full of secret hide-outs for us. Turning in through the big entrance gates from the road, a lawn — our croquet lawn — lay on the right of the drive surrounded by a mixed shrubbery of evergreens and lilacs, laburnums and pink Mays. There was also a guelder rose with hanging white bobbles and a hugh philadelphus, syringa as we quite wrongly called it which breathed out the most heavenly scent. Just outside the old oak porch over the front door which had once in its life sheltered the lych gate to a church, stood an enormous cedar, its long octopus-like branches almost touching the porch. I can never see a cedar without thinking of Colonel Broome.

Colonel Broome was an old friend of grandpapa Cook, and was often included in the coach parties which grandpapa drove over from Richmond where he lived in order to see us and to show off the whole outfit for our delight. On one of these visits, as we all crowded round admiring the four superb bays tossing their heads (they wore bearing reins poor things, of course, and threw froth all over their necks) mingling with the beautifully dressed crowd in picture hats, long skirts, grey suits and toppers, I was startled to hear my name called twice in a raucous parrotty voice, 'Vera, Vera'! Could there really be a parrot somewhere in the trees, how truly wonderful! So thought I in my foolish innocence, looking up eagerly into the heavy greenery, when suddenly I caught sight of a crouching figure behind the cedar and saw Colonel Broome resplendent in a pale grey suit, hiding his face behind his straw boater. 'Vera, Vera' he squawked into the boater and the roar of laughter that went up from the gallant company only added to my mortification. What a fool I had been made to look and how I hated Colonel Broome.

On the other side of the house lay another and a bigger lawn in the middle of which was a stone fountain continually spattering water onto broad, flat lily leaves. On to these lily leaves one day Rachel, then about two, fell with a loud splash; she had been standing on the edge trying to reach the upper storey where the stone boy held the serpent spouting water. Luckily mother, Olga and I were not far off and, as the dripping, yelling figure was carried into the house, I sadly surveyed the scene of carnage. The only undamaged thing seemed to be Rachel's enormous straw hat floating on the water — above the smashed lilies and tangled leaves.

There was a nut-walk beneath an avenue of hazel trees, a midget path meandering through a rather soggy Dutch garden known as the 'wilderness'. And, of course, we had 'houses' all over the garden, the biggest one being in the enormous rhododendron bush sprawling magnificently at the end of the music-room.

Card, *Mr.* Card to us, was at one and the same time our respected friend and enemy. He was 'king' of the garden and, of course, everything in it was his. If we kept to the rules, he was friendly and all smiles, but if we were caught picking a flower or fruit without permission or walking across his 'beds' he would report us to Nannie who in turn reported us to mother. I was very fond of Card in spite of falling foul of him sometimes. He was a tiny, little man with a Vandyke beard and twinkling eyes. In fact, the whole Card family was miniature, Mrs. Card, daughter Minnie, and son Arthur.

I can well remember that day when Olga and I succumbed to the lure of fat, ripe gooseberries dangling on the bushes behind the herbaceous border; we were about four and five. Suddenly, nannie's voice smote upon our ears and guiltily clutching the, as yet, uneaten fruit in our hot hands, we stood with them hidden behind our backs, an idiotic thing to do for nobody could have failed to notice our confusion. Card was well within earshot and, resting on his spade, was preparing to enjoy the little drama. And drama it certainly was, for nannie, not being a fool, demanded to see our hands. Caught red-handed, or gooseberry-handed, there was nothing we could do but drop the things onto the path behind us. I shall never forget my humiliation knowing that Card had witnessed my shame. This was a far greater punishment than anything nannie could have devised. I avoided him for some while afterwards, being afraid he must have a very poor opinion of me.

Card looked after the electric-light engine installed by Father. There was no grid then and until we had that engine we had to make do with lamps and candles. This engine (Petter, I believe) was a huge affair with two big fly wheels and a black flapping belt. At intervals during the day the peace was shattered by its poppings and thumpings. Of course, we were forbidden to go into the engine room and rightly too, nor into the battery house adjoining, which was full of exciting looking glass tanks with bubbling liquid and a queer smell.

I think it was fairly soon after its installation that the engine back-fired one day with disastrous results. Engine room, battery house, stabling and Card's cottage caught fire and were burnt to the ground. We were having tea (a rare occurence) that day with some friends in Oxshott when somebody noticed black smoke rising from the direction of Copseham. We hurried home to find the place in pandemonium, fire-engines all over the place, blind-folded horses being led out of the stables and all Card's precious belongings scattered over the lawn outside their cottage. And that was the end of electric light for a while.

Our days passed quietly enough in the simple nursery regime. When we were considered able to walk the six miles to Esher and back, which was when Olga and I were about nine and ten, we would set out, nannie pushing the baby Francis, in his pram; the nursery maid Rachel, in a kind of basket-work go-cart; while Olga and I trudged alongside. Arriving in the High Street, nannie did the round energetically. We would always go to Mr. Chapman, the chemist, for such necessary horrors as Grey powders (one every Saturday night, in case), later to be superseded by Syrup of figs, just as nasty; but mainly for nannie's bottle of Hall's wine which appeared to be absolutely essential to her welfare. It looked like port and we were quite sure nannie sat in the rocking chair every evening when we were in bed downing glass after glass. Of course, we realised later that it was only a harmless medicinal wine with no potent effects like port. We were fond of Mr. Chapman with his shiny, bald head for he would never forget to give us a welcome acid-drop. Another shop I can remember well, because I hated going there, was Mr. Style's, the draper's, because it smelt of castor-oil and I couldn't bear the sound of tearing calico. Having done all the shopping, we set off on the long walk home again.

About a mile beyond the Village, for Esher was hardly more than that then, the road passed the entrance gates to Claremont, home of the widowed Duchess of Albany. This was where in 1817, George IV's daughter, the Princess Charlotte, had died in childbirth. At the lodge gates stood a very smart figure in a green tail coat with shining buttons and a top hat with cockade. I always thought that smart person was the Duchess, no one having told me what a duchess was. But I was rudely jolted from my romantic dreams when, at some function which the Duchess was to open, Olga and I had to present her with a bouquet. To my immense surprise and disappointment, instead of the beautiful gentleman in top hat and tails, a stout, dumpy, old lady in a·black silk dress and a black bonnet stooped over our curtsying little figures and gave us each a kiss.

Social do's like that were rare occurrences. Even children's parties were only permitted reluctantly for fear of infection, and it was surprising that the weekly dancing classes were not tabooed for the same reason. I suppose these were considered a necessary risk in the interests of education. At any rate, dancing class day was for me a red letter day.

We went with nannie to the Esher Village Hall in the brougham driven by our dear Robert. The brougham was a smart affair in navy blue with our coat of arms on the door panel. Inside there was room for two grown-ups and a small child on the main seat and there was a funny little stool-like seat opposite which was usually folded up, but which could be unfolded and raised upon its one leg and used as an extra. The inside of the carriage smelt of polish and horse and leather, and it ran smoothly on its four rubber-tyred wheels. The only sounds to be heard as we drove along were the clip-clop of the horse's hooves on the road, the squeaking of springs and leather and the jingle of bits. In cold weather we were given a footwarmer and fur rugs. The window, or 'glass' as Fanny Burney would have called it, one on either side, could be raised or lowered by a leather strap. We were never allowed to sit on the box beside Robert and I was never allowed to drive the brougham as I was the dog-cart and pony trap.

Arriving at the village hall, which looks exactly the same today (outside at any rate) as it did then, more than sixty years ago, we joined the large mixed class of children under the enthusiastic direction of Miss Wright and her assistant, not forgetting the poor wilting pianist forever thumping out the same old tunes on the ancient, out-of-tune piano. Everyone wore their best dresses and suits and I, for one, enjoyed every minute of the afternoon for in dancing I could come out of my shell. Indeed, I can quite truthfully say I was one of the best. I waited with madly beating heart for the expected summons. 'Vera Cook, will you please come into the front row.' There I was called upon to demonstrate a step or a movement, conscious of a multitude of eyes staring at me. I could skip well, too, and was once given a box of chocolates for doing the 'double through' more times than anybody else. I was never in any danger of getting a swelled head, for if ever a child needed encouragement it was I, for I was shy and hesitant with little self-confidence. I knew I could never sparkle as my sister could and, though over four years younger than I, Rachel was never slow in keeping me in a back seat. How horrid children can be to each other; the old Adam was very active in all us dear little souls.

I can remember there was one small girl we all hated simply because we were envious of her beautiful sausage curls which bounced up and down when she danced. I don't think we realised this was the puerile reason for our enmity; we thought she was swanky, so we set on her like a pack of terriers on a rat. Every time she passed by us in a dance and we happened to be sitting out on the chairs round the hall, we would try to give her a sly pinch or if, as sometimes happened, she was our partner in a dance, we squeezed her hand as hard and as long as we could and stepped on her toes. This treatment she bore in stoic silence so we got little satisfaction out of that. I don't expect we squeezed or stamped hard enough to hurt much.

We made friends with several of the children to the extent of going out to tea with them. I remember one boy called Jacob Bright who sported a black velvet suit with a lace collar. We scorned him. There were Micky Virtue and his sister, and John and Eileen Cobb, all of whom we liked; John eventually became the famous car-racing driver later to be killed on Coniston Water.

After an afternoon with skipping ropes, garlands and Indian clubs, we finished up learning to waltz, polka and gallop. Then, hot and tired, but happy, we found Robert and the brougham waiting for us outside (no parking metres or yellow lines) and were driven home.

Cars meant nothing to us in those days. It was horses, coaches, carriages and all the paraphernalia connected with them. We played 'horses' on our walks, taking it in turns to be driver and driven. The driven wore a harness of red, knitted wool, home-made, but I can also remember a leather breastplate covered with jangling bells. The driver carried a long whip and that was the more coveted role. Olga as the elder usually managed to bag it. At an election we donned enormous rosettes of yellow and purple, the Tory colours, and pinned ribbons to whip and harness. There was a similar excitement over the Boat Race which we never saw as children. Father being a Balliol man we were all for the dark blues and smothered ourselves in dark blue everything, even to our underwear. Any glimpse of Cambridge blue was like a red rag to a bull. Trotting along the dusty roads playing horses or bowling our wooden hoops was a far nicer form of constitutional than the modern child can indulge in because then there was only an occasional cart or carriage to send us scuttling to the side of the road and it was a very leisurely scuttle with nothing doing much more than ten miles per hour.

A great joy was the visit of the organ grinder and his little monkey. Why he chose to wander along the long road between Esher and us I don't know, but come he did, and we rushed to see him in great excitement. How I loved that barrel organ and the dark-eyed Italian smilingly grinding out the thumping metallic music. The poor old organ from age and years of exposure to all weathers had a sort of hesitancy in delivering its tunes like a hoarse musical stammer, but I adored it and would stand spell-bound at the gate listening and staring. I can remember putting a penny, rather timidly into the monkey's cold little hand held out to us, but I can't remember giving it anything to eat; I hope we did. It wore a red flannel frock and a little cap with elastic under its chin. I was not troubled about the welfare of monkeys in those days and I suppose, provided they had kind masters and enough food and warmth, that sort of life was preferable to sitting in a cage, bored to death. I expect it would have been a Capuchin monkey for they quickly learn tricks. I can hardly believe it would have lasted out a cold winter and would most probably have died of pneumonia.

Perhaps the most exciting thing that came our way on our outings was the possibility of meeting a certain lady who lived further up the road towards Oxshott. She was a Mrs Despard, a militant suffragette. Occasionally the even more

Myself

Mother, myself and Rachel
1907

Francis, 1920

My father, 1924 (*by Sir William Orpen R.A.*)

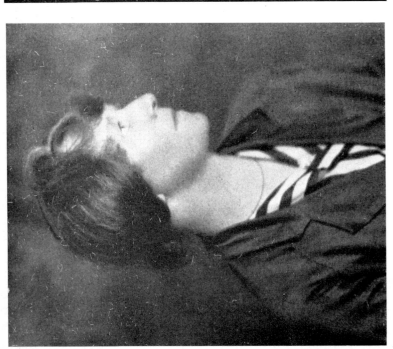

My mother

notorious Mrs. Pankhurst and her daughter, Christabel, came to stay with her. An aura of disapproval hung around that house, why we never understood – all we could think was that Mrs. Despard must be a witch. Nannie hurried us past the little house as though it were a fever hospital with germs jumping out of it, forbidding us to stare. If, as occasionally happened, we met Mrs. Despard on the road and there could be no turning back, nannie put on her most disapproving expression with never a glance to left or right and dragged us past as fast as we could go. From surreptitious glances beneath lowered eyes we were agreeably surprised at the witch's appearance. She had shining white hair which shone through a flowing black chiffon veil and sandalled feet peeped from beneath long voluminous black skirts; really most attractive, for a witch. But nannie thought otherwise; in her opinion Mrs. Despard, whatever she was, was a very dangerous person.

4

Father –
A Very Special Kind of Draper

For years we accepted the fact that father worked in the City without having the least idea what he did there. We knew it must be something very important because the whole home routine revolved around his activities.

The day began with family prayers at eight o'clock, followed by breakfast. At nine o'clock father went off to catch the 9.15 to Waterloo and the day ended with him being met at the station at 6.0 p.m. and arriving home in time to bid us goodnight. We saw more of him at week-ends, and as we grew older when we sometimes played a game of croquet with him on summer evenings before we went to bed. As for that mysterious place called 'The City' which swallowed up father every day and from whence he returned every evening tired and smelling of stuffy trains, we only knew that it was where the 'firm' was. That the 'firm' was in a churchyard seemed a bit puzzling. It was only when we began going to London to the dentist or photographer or to see the Lord Mayor's Show and went to lunch at Cook, Son and Co., Warehousemen, 22 St. Paul's Churchyard that the veil began to lift.

We decided that Father must be a draper, but, of course, a very special kind of draper although he didn't seem to do anything half as exciting as our Mr. Styles did in his draper's shop in Esher High Street. Father didn't walk up and down between the counters with hands under his coat-tails bowing and smiling, neither did he lean over a counter to rip calico from top to bottom with a screech to set my teeth a-jangle; no, Father must have had a much, much duller day, of that we were sure, having sometimes witnessed some of his activities in the warehouse.

When we were taken to that hive of industry in the Churchyard we were first of all ushered into father's dark, little office smelling of mouldy books and stuffy leather chairs. It had very grimy windows through which I could just make out the odd shapes of other people's chimneys. We thought it a nasty place and felt sorry for father having to sit there all day long. He looked, in his morning suit just as smart as Mr. Styles and it seemed to me a great pity that he was not taking a more active part in the shop, instead of being hidden away all the time. I, myself, considered father outshone Mr. Styles in every respect, not only because he looked so tall and smelt so nice, but because he had a gold chain looped across his waistcoat front, which Mr. Styles had not. At one end of this chain was the wonderful gold half-hunter watch with its magic lid which opened when we blew upon it. At the other end of the chain was a silver sovereign case in which father kept golden sovereigns and ten shilling pieces which popped up when one pressed the slide which kept them in place. Hooked onto this chain, the money end was a pair of minute, collapsible nail-scissors. Father's hands were thin and flat with long fingers and always very clean. When he bent down to kiss us he smelt deliciously of violet hair-oil. The only thing I did not like much was the scratching of his small, ginger moustache.

Father's day began quite colourfully, even though the middle part must have been boring, or so it seemed to us. After family prayers and breakfast, Robert, the coachman, brought the carriage to the door at nine o'clock precisely. Father was always punctual, sometimes embarrassingly so when, as occasionally happened, he was a shade ahead of the stated time. I cannot remember his ever being late. If prayers were scheduled for 8 a.m. then 8 a.m. meant prayers; father would be in his place ready and expected everyone else to be likewise. It was a bit of a bind sometimes but I think the discipline of that upbringing did us no harm. In fact, I find it harder to be late than punctual, even at my age. So, at 9 a.m. precisely, there was the brougham, if wet, or the dog-cart, if fine, waiting outside the little porch. Father would drive the dog-cart himself and liked me to do the same when I was older.

The two horses I remember best and which were sometimes used as a pair in the brougham were a fine bay called Exploit and a young rather clumsy thing called Jumbo which father liked to drive in the dog-cart. Exploit had once been one of grandpapa Cook's coach horses. He was beginning to age a bit and so had been handed on to us as a reliable, intelligent old trusty, good for many more years of less arduous work. He lived to a great age and had perfect manners which is more than can be said of Jumbo. Jumbo was young and heavy with enormous feet and a hard mouth. He never could or would behave normally nor stand quietly waiting for his passengers, like old Exploit did. Directly father appeared in the porch pulling on his brown kid gloves, Jumbo would see him from the corner of his rolling eye. Up he would go on his hind legs, pawing the air with his front ones like a circus turn, much to Robert's discomforture, for he, poor chap, was supposed to be holding Jumbo steady while father climbed onto the box, but more often was to be seen suspended in the air, top hat awry but still hanging on courageously. Father remained calm, showing no emotion or surprise. During a pause in the performance he would suddenly step nimbly onto the dog-cart and as soon as he had gathered the reins and picked up his whip Jumbo and Robert resumed more normal positions and off the carriage dashed leaving poor Robert running after it down the drive. Before it reached the entrance gate Robert had caught up with it and would have managed to swing himself up onto the back seat by the hand grips. There he would dust himself down, straighten hat and coat and assume a dignified position, arms folded across chest, elbows out and white-breached knees apart. Then with a grin and a wink to us watching the entertainment, he was whirled out of our sight. I suppose father must have known what was going on behind his back but he never, by look or remark, showed that he did.

Robert remained like that, sitting smartly to attention all the two miles or so to Oxshott station, then, as though eager to show how much he enjoyed acrobatics, he would leap off the cart which was still going full speed and race alongside Jumbo so as to be at his head directly he stopped. And father, flinging down the reins stepped down quickly before Jumbo had time to begin any of his tricks. With a smile and 'meet me six-thirty, Robert', father disappeared into the booking office. When I was older and could drive father to and from the station, Robert Blakey always came with me to give the right touch of smartness to the turn-out.

Dear Robert, he had bright Irish blue eyes and was kindness itself teaching me the art of riding and driving. He went to France late in the 1914 War with the Veterinary Corps, and he and his horses were blown to bits in their billets one night.

I remember feeling so sorry for him sitting up on the driving box in bad weather, wrapped in a big waterproof cape, the rain pouring off his glistening top hat, over his face and down his neck. He always remained cheerful, accepting the cold and wet as ungrumblingly as the hottest summer sun. Coachmen were a hardy race with nothing to protect them from the rain except their capes and waterproof aprons and no awning to shield them from the sun. We had our share of the weather, too, rain or too much sun when out in the wagonette, dog-cart or pony-trap, so we could sympathize with Robert's trials.

The last pony that I can remember was called Flue, not because it flew along (which, in fact, it did) but because we were indulging in 'flu when it was bought. The Flue Cart had two very large wheels and was shaped like a 'U', the driver sitting in the loop of the 'U'. Unless other bodies were in the cart making it more level, the poor pony always seemed in danger of being lifted off its legs. I was not encouraged, though never actually forbidden, to drive this outfit because Flue was considered somewhat of a handful for me, but I usually managed to persuade Robert to let me take the reins. Once, when going out to tea with some friends in Cobham (I must have been about twelve, I think) I had coaxed Robert to let me drive and we were bowling along at a spanking trot, the roads being still pleasantly empty, when we were overtaken by one of the still rather rare motor-cars. As it passed us and Flue nervously broke into a canter, its occupant, an old man with a shock of snowy hair leant forward in his seat and waved to us, smiling gaily. It was the great Lloyd George! I suppose it must have amused him to see me wrestling with the mettlesome Flue. Robert and I felt honoured, but as I was not really supposed to be driving, I could say nothing about the incident when I returned home, which was disappointing.

Coming back to father. I imagine the rest of the day when he got home was comparatively peaceful, but until I was old enough to be included in some of the evening events I can only guess what went on. I know there were dinner parties with music and billiards afterwards; friends often came to stay and in the light summer evenings, trying in vain to go to sleep I would lie and listen with enjoyment to the sounds of laughter and singing and piano music floating into my open windows.

There were other evenings sometimes when father had been kept late in London, perhaps a committee meeting or an exhibition at his club, the Burlington Fine Arts, or he might just shut himself into his library and write; for beside his drapery activities, father was a distinguished art critic and connoisseur and the author of several books.

With mother he shared a great love of music, as well as

being a good pianist himself. I listened to them playing
duets – Beethoven, Haydn, Mozart and Schubert. The day
would come when I would be doing the same but with father
only; mother preferred to strum her own compositions. She
did not read music as well as he, nor had she the same
pleasure in the classics, nor the ability to play them. But
what she lacked in technique and professionalism was more
than accounted for by the warmth and liveliness of her
interpretations. Tchaikowsky at one time was a hot favourite,
so was Rachmaninoff, and the place resounded to portions of
their concertos played on piano, concertina or even whistled.

Mother was quite professional with her concertina, an
English concertina, which is much more classy and far harder
to play than the usual 'squeeze box' type. Father and I were
often called upon to play the accompaniments for her to
pieces she liked; very often sonatas for violin or 'cello. There
was never a lack of music of all kinds. I was certainly brought
up to the 'sound of music', real live music, most of which we
made ourselves. We did have a gramephone, seldom played
except in holiday time at Studland when we were older.

We all became, as befitted well brought-up young Edward-
ians, experts at croquet, playing it on every possible occasion.
And what a pleasant form of amusement it was, with no
undue exertion to reduce one to an unbecoming shade of
crimson and with no special outfit to don; in fact, one could
and did play in one's Sunday best, if necessary. Father loved
his croquet, too; he was a good all round games player, but
mother only played most dutifully a kind of social croquet
with friends who needed entertaining. Tennis succeeded
croquet, but we children were not allowed to play that till
much later on; anyhow the croquet lawn was hardly adequate
for a full-sized tennis court, so father eventually bought some
land at the other end of the common. On this, and without
any planning permission, he built a laundry which housed
two washer-women and all the necessary accoutrement; a
cottage for Marjorie Johnson, Wag as we always called her,

one of our parents' oldest and dearest friends; a large wooden bungalow which we used for our photographic experiments and geological collection; a hard tennis court and a vegetable garden to supplement the inadequate garden. There was also a revolving summer house in which we did our lessons. There is a story attached to this venerable edifice, for it is still very much alive, after a varied career of some sixty or more years.

Built by Bolton and Paul, a firm renowned for the excellence of its work, it spent many years of its later life as a real summer house in the garden of our holiday home in Studland where Father, by then a victim of that cruel affliction, paralysis agitans, almost permanently lived. He could not stand the increasing pace and brashness of life and found the little Voysey-built stone-roofed house overlooking the shining sea a real haven of peace. He would rest a great deal and always in the old summer house, which standing as it did upon its revolving base, could follow the sun as it travelled across the heavens. Later still, after father died and the War had ended and I and my family had returned to our home, the summer-house came with us. Today it stands in our garden, but now it is fixed on its base, slightly altered inside. However it is much the same outside and looking cheerful and debonair in spite of its fall in social status. For it is now a home for my monkeys. Why this should be considered in any way degrading seems hard to explain, but the fact that once upon a time it had seen better days (or so it is said) invariably raises pitying smiles on the face of the onlookers.

Well, when this ancient building was in its hey-day and was placed in the field overlooking the tennis court at Copseham we were expected to study therein. Of course we greatly enjoyed this setting for our lessons, as conversely our long-suffering governess hated it. For how could one concentrate on sums and such-like horrors while in our ears sounded so many disturbing and delightful noises of the great out-of-doors, not least the shouts and laughter of father and his friends enjoying a game of tennis on Saturday morning when we still had a morning's work to do?

I went sometimes to Hampton Court with father to watch him play real tennis in the old Tudor covered wooden court. It seemed to me, understanding nothing about the art of tennis, much less the real old kind, the noisiest and most energetic of games. I was breathless with admiration for father's energy and antics (he was a first class player) and applauded him enthusiastically.

At golf and billiards he was an above average player, and in both these games he coached me as soon as he considered me capable of wielding a club and careful enough to be trusted with a cue. He took these lessons very seriously, so did I; in fact, I somewhat dreaded them. Father was not one to suffer fools gladly, but was generous in his praise if he saw I was really trying; fooling about was never allowed. As I got older, in my teens, I managed to give my demanding parent quite a good game of billiards with a handicap that got less and less as I improved. But I can't remember ever winning. These games were an ordeal, exciting but alarming because of the ever present fear of 'cutting the cloth'. This dreadful possibility hung over my head like an axe poised to descend. Thank goodness it never happened. The billiard room was oak-panelled with a large tapestry covered chest one end. Otherwise it was entirely filled with the three-quarter length table – covered with a golden brown damask cloth. It was my job to get everything ready for our game at the given hour so I turned on the four big round hanging lights over the table, folded up the cloth, placing it neatly on a small table. I put the three ivory billiard balls where they should be, then sat waiting on the big seat. Punctual to the minute, father appeared, selected his cue, chose one he considered right for me, and the game began. If we had an audience it was expected to maintain silence except for discreet applause or sympathetic sighs.

When father was feeling too tired for billiards, he might

ask me to play to him. This amounted to a royal command and I never dreamt of refusing. By the time I was about twelve I had become a good pianist for my age and loved playing but found these demands from my critical, though always appreciative, parent a little daunting; I was so afraid of disappointing him. But soon my shyness melted away in the sheer joy of playing on that Steinway. What a marvellous instrument it was; I have never ever played on a finer. What a contrast to the schoolroom upright on which I practised and the poor wornout old crocks I struggled with during my four years at boarding school. The Steinway spoke in velvet tones, just to lay my fingers on the keys almost took my breath away and the fact that it was *my* fingers which produced such sounds never failed to amaze me.

Sunday was very much father's day. Perhaps it was because we saw so little of him during the week that Sunday's programme remains so clear to me. First of all there was the morning service in Esher Church. Sometimes when it was very fine father walked us there and back, partly because he did not like bringing Robert out on Sunday after his strenuous week-day work and partly because he liked the exercise. But sometimes, if it looked like rain, Robert did come to fetch us back in the pony cart, for which we were grateful. At other times Father himself drove us to church in the pony cart, stabled the thing at the 'Bear Hotel' and drove us home again after the service. Dressed in our best, we assembled in the porch ready for father. Mother's dress sense was decidedly original, as were all her other ideas. We went through periods of fashions or crazes and whatever else our clothing was, it was never like anyone else's. This did not worry me at all till much later when I noticed curious glances cast upon me and began to realise they were not so much of admiration as of amusement.

In our very early days we wore frills and lace, mostly white and everything was hand-made; I can well remember watching nannie 'scalloping' round the bottom of my flannel petticoat. Of course we wore far too many clothes; combinations, flannel bodice, linings and drawers, flannel petticoat, white petticoat and frock and a pinafore to keep the latter clean. Later the crazes began, sailor suits being one of the first. Navy serge skirts and sailor blouses for week days, all white for Sunday with stiff straw hats with HMS something or other on the hat bands. Mine was HMS *Victory* of which I felt proud. Mother was a *Hood* and Admiral Lord Nelson my mother's great-great uncle. So in a way I felt I did have a little right to advertise my illustrious ancestor. The rest of the outfit was hardly up to his standard, I fear, with white button boots, black silk kerchief, lanyard and whistle. In very hot weather we wore holland overalls almost down to our boots but these were comfortable; the only objection I had was that they were stiff and smelt like the castor-oil smell in Mr. Style's shop which I disliked.

There was a truly awful period when a creature called Buster Brown in some book or magazine was all the rage. He had a dog called Tighe. This child was dressed in tunics and shorts with a belt low down under the tummy, a hard white collar and a bow tie. We were little Buster Browns for quite a while. Djibbers were another fashion and were rather nice. They were made, as far as I can remember, of heavy silk with flower motifs in brilliant colours. Mine was kingfisher blue with bunches of iris on my chest. I really rather liked it. I can remember our winter coats well. Both Olga and I had bright red ones with brass buttons, but again Olga was one up on me, having a small black velvet collar on hers. We had white felt hats with ostrich plumes and tied under the chin with a broad satin ribbon. Our best summer hats delighted me, they were of yellowish straw and had a wreath of buttercups and forget-me-nots round the crown.

Thus adorned in one of the aforesaid outfits, not forgetting our cotton or kid gloves, we set off on the long walk with father. I never remember mother coming with us. I do not think she liked walking because of her varicose veins.

The organist of Esher Church was Montague Phillips, a distinguished musician and a great family friend. We called him David and his wife, Clara Butterworth, we called Phillipa. They were frequent visitors at Copseham and many delightful hours we spent listening to Phillipa's splendid voice and to David's playing which miraculously charmed away father's 'blues'. We listened entranced to them both, labouring to bring to birth the *Lilac Domino* and the *Rebel Maid* in both of which operettas Phillipa was to distinguish herself in the London productions.

Long before 'The Fishermen of England' became known to the great British public we were singing with gusto that stirring chorus. What splendid fun we had.

David, from long experience of father's taste in music would have prepared a suitable programme to play for him after the Sunday service was over. When the Church was empty, except for other friends like ourselves who knew what was coming, we settled down expectantly for a feast of music. We were never disappointed, for David was a very fine organist. The moment for which we children had been waiting came with the first notes of the 'Prize Song' from Wagner's *Die Meistersinger*. We immediately turned our heads to gaze at father who never failed to come up to our expectations. When moved with pleasurable emotion father breathed heavily, his nostrils flapped in and out, his eyes became suspiciously moist and I imagine he had a lump in the throat. The 'Prize Song' never failed to produce these signs of ecstasy which, I regret to say, reduced us to delighted but well controlled giggles.

I can never think back to those Sundays at Copseham without feelings of guilt and remorse. We had an Old English sheepdog who belonged to no one in particular. This poor animal was chained day and night to his kennel in the garden. If we remembered we took him for a walk with us, otherwise he spent his life straining at his chain and barking continuously. However often we failed him, father never forget him at week-ends. Rufus's excitement when he saw father approaching reached fever pitch and there was a struggle to unfasten the chain from the collar of the bounding bundle of grey and white energy leaping up and down trying to lick our faces, which token of affection we little deserved. Animals, as pets, were not encouraged, why I don't know; I suppose neither parent was interested. Mother, later, had a succession of small dogs, skipperkees I think they were called, and two marmosets which eventually were given to the Zoo or died. Greatly daring, I once managed to acquire a small tabby cat which I called Smutty. When it inevitably produced kittens I was so afraid that because of this shameful event it would be taken away from me, that I screwed up my courage and my eyes and drowned the hour-old little things in a bucket of water in the stable yard. Naturally, such a thing as that did not pass unnoticed. The reaction to it was quite the opposite to what I had expected; *I* was accused of being a cruel murderess and Smutty, the bereaved mother, became the object of everybody's sympathy. I often ponder on the injustice of such things because I am perfectly convinced had I not done the deed Smutty would have been taken away from me because of her immorality.

5

Edwardian Household

◆━━◆

Etiquette among the staff of an Edwardian household was rigid and important. The entire menage was modelled on the old feudal system. Thus the cook who was queen of the lower regions, of the kitchen in particular, was almost expected to bully the kitchen-maid who in turn pitched into the scullery-maid. Naturally there were degrees of bullying, some bearable and good humoured, some the opposite. The same charming system prevailed in the pantry department with the butler or parlourmaid as 'pitcher-in-chief'; likewise among the housemaids. I well remember my feeling of guilt one day having caught a glimpse of a girl, not much older than I was myself then, with sleeves rolled up, on hands and knees scrubbing the stone floors in the kitchen. I fervently hoped she hadn't seen me on my way to the croquet lawn to enjoy myself. But was life below stairs really so awful?

In the opinions of the old die-hards who have survived those tyranical times and enjoy looking back to the 'good old days', life could have been a lot worse and, in some respects, couldn't have been better. There was plenty of food, gossip and scandal and a good bust up now and then relieved the monotony of the well regulated hours.

In the pantry we sometimes had a parlourmaid when butlers were scarce, which wasn't often. Father really preferred a butler. Mother certainly did, especially after the episode with Miss Wilson. No harm meant on either side, but surely father could have found a slightly less conspicuous opponent on the local golf course than his dashing parlour-maid with the flaming red hair, even though she could give him such a good game?

I remember two of the butlers well. One was called Pike and he had a sour, square, yellow face. His wife was the cook. Then there was Bliss, tall, dark and good-looking. He was unmarried, the cook then being a Mrs. Dainty. Bliss and Dainty came in for many a caustic and witty comment from father, out of earshot of course. There was a page-boy invariably called Albert, clad in navy blue bum-freezers in winter and white ditto in summer. Rows of silver buttons ran down his front. These Alberts came and went with monotonous regularity either to better themselves by becoming a footman elsewhere, or because they couldn't stand the pantry discipline, and sometimes because we couldn't stand them. Sometimes we had a footman as well, probably when a lot of entertaining was going on; we then borrowed one of Grandpapa Cook's. Of course he wore tails and a red waistcoat and on his coat were silver buttons with the family crest. He was far smarter and grander looking than the butler who wore plain black. We had no more than a nodding acquaintance with the scullery-maids and the Alberts; nannie would have considered it most infra-dig if we had made friends with them. Nannie undoubtedly was a snob.

Now we come to the two most important departments of the household as far as I was concerned, namely the nursery and the schoolroom. When Olga joined the family, nannie Simmonds took over from my first nannie. She soon had Rachel, my sister, to cope with and later my brother Francis. In addition, there was always an under-nurse to help look after us and a young nursery-maid to clean the nurseries and wait on the lot. I had always carried a picture in my mind right up to the day I was married of an austere person in a stiff and starched white frock and apron or perhaps a pale grey coat and skirt with black bonnet on Sundays, so that I was somewhat surprised when nannie turned up as a guest at

(*above*) Copseham, Esher; (*below*) Sir Frederick and Lady Cook with my father (holding coach-horn), his two sisters and friends on the coach-and-four. About 1896

Sir Frederick Cook, 2nd Bart, 1924; (*right*) Col. Arthur Wellington
Alexander Nelson Hood, 2nd Viscount Bridport

My aunt, the Hon. Sybil Hood in her first Standard car. About 1911
(A 'Brownie' snap taken by me)

the wedding reception and I found myself looking down from my considerable height of five feet two upon a tiny little figure with a beaming wrinkled face. Nannie was always kind to me; we got on well and it never struck me that her treatment of poor Olga was any different.

Olga being the older was invariably blamed for all misdeeds and for leading me astray. I was quite oblivious of this fact as also that nannie resented her inclusion in the nursery circle. I fear she never missed the opportunity of reminding poor Olga of the transgressions not only of her parents, but of her grandparents. I suppose there must always be a risk of unfair treatment when someone else's child is taken into a family and especially in the days of nannies, who were often over-zealous, narrow-minded and dreadfully snobbish. I am sure mother never realised how nannie could, and did, bully Olga at times, for the nursery was very much on its own and nannie reigned supreme. Olga and I were always good friends, becoming more so after Rachel and then Francis were born. By that time we were of course beginning to embark on our schoolroom careers.

As far as one is able to form an opinion of one's self as a child from remarks, complimentary or otherwise, let fall by relations and friends and by photographs, I seem to have been quite a pretty child with reddish curls, round pink face and wide open enquiring eyes. I must have been quite a dull little thing though, content to play with my family of dolls and only asking to be left in peace. For some reason I lacked self-confidence and was very sensitive to reproof and disapproval. I bit my nails and developed a stammer, both of which failings became heavy burdens throughout my school life. I retired still further into my shell when my sister came onto the footlights, for she had all the sparkle and confidence I lacked; therefore I became accustomed to playing second fiddle in practically everything. Rachel loved Teddy bears, dolls were sickly things in her opinion; she was made of much sterner stuff than I was and mother adored her.

I grew quickly up to the age of twelve and had long thin legs and flat feet. Because of this mother insisted on encasing them in boots; white button boots, brown and black laced boots, but never shoes, even for indoors. I accepted this without rancour until I began going to school. Mother could have had no idea the torture I endured having to wear boots indoors when everybody else wore shoes. Flat-footed or not, I was always able to dance and jump as well as, and sometimes better than most. There is a photo in the book of mother, Rachel and myself taken when I was seven and Rachel three. I look subdued (not unusual) and rather tight lipped. This was because mother had forbidden me to smile or open my mouth while being photographed because I had just lost my two top front teeth. This catastrophe had come upon me that very day. During the drive through London to the photographer, Rachel had flipped her hand across my mouth to stop me talking and my teeth had fallen into my lap; I must admit they had been hanging on threads for some while.

Another cross I had to bear was my hair, or my lack of it. When quite small I had fine reddish curls. By degrees it got duller and darker till it looked like the proverbial rat's tails. The edict then went forth that it must all be cut off to strengthen its growth. Olga and Rachel lost their curls, too, and we went around with close cropped heads like convicts. Before mother lost patience with the wretched stuff, nannie would curl it up in rags every night in a desperate attempt to make me look attractive. How I hated this, because I never could find a smooth place on the pillow on which to lay my head. For an hour or so next day I would appear with beautiful corkscrew curls but they soon went. I was rising nine when Francis was born but the event did not make such a great impression on me because by then Olga and I had embarked on the exciting, if not always enjoyable, adventure of schoolroom life.

The nursery considered itself vastly superior to the

schoolroom and indeed, to all other departments; after all, nannie and her retinue had been functioning for years before a schoolroom came into being and this new regime, involving the care and training of her charges by someone else, was a state of affairs hardly to be tolerated. It very seldom was. Here we could feel the pull; in fact we felt almost criminal when after breakfast nannie sent us down to the schoolroom with acid comments about 'that Miss – ' whoever she happened to be at that time. Every wretched governess started work under a severe handicap with nannie's eagle eye upon her, claws and beak tearing her to bits at every opportunity. A long procession of them came and went . . . nannie remained.

The very first governess was a Miss Brooks, young, fair and pretty but no match for nannie. Miss Dalton, one of the next fascinated us and seriously handicapped our progress because we couldn't help staring at the two black hairs which sprouted from a pimple on her chin. Wondering why she had them and how they got there was a much more engrossing train of thought than the multiplication table. There was Miss Barcham, masculine and hearty with black boots, hard collar and deep voice. I would have thought she might have been a match for nannie, but no, she soon departed. And the attractive Miss Wilkinson. I can see her now, floating languidly down the oak stairway into the music room to join us for family prayers, the sunbeams slanting through the window lighting up her silvery hair, her complexion like peaches and cream, her periwinkle blue eyes gazing innocently at her admiring audience and her long earrings swinging backwards and forwards against her neck. Even we, in spite of her mild tyranny in the schoolroom thought her very pretty. Father obviously did; mother rather more doubtfully and nannie positively bristled with disapproval. Soon Miss Wilkinson was on her way.

When we were older our schoolroom classes were increased by several other daily pupils and we also had a series of

Mademoiselles. Our knowledge of the French language benefited greatly but because we were expected to converse in French when we lunched in the dining-room with our parents and their friends I began to get a complex about the language and became idiotically dumb when a well-meaning parent or visitor tossed some quite puerile and inoffensive remark to me in French. Tears of mortification and fright mingled with the food I was trying to gulp down but for the life of me, I could not utter '*un mot*'. Ultimately, we reached a good enough standard to act scenes from the French classics for our parents' entertainment at the end of term.

Punishments were all too frequent, especially after our umpteenth governess, Miss Lowell, had been installed. Due to her canine characteristics of snapping, and barking at us for the smallest misdemeanour she was immediately labelled 'Bow-wow' by our sympathetic though rather naughty American friend, Chester Fentress (Hennie, we called him). Bow-wow's dragonian programme included a backboard covered with green baize on which we had to stretch out, one could hardly call it 'rest' for half an hour after lunch. It was hard and uncompromising but it did have a shallow scoop for our heads. Much worse than this mild form of torture were the braces or shoulder straps into which we were forced. These delightful aids to deportment cut into our arms and shoulders if we bent too low over our work bringing us upright with cruel urgency.

For one thing, only, do I feel grateful to Bow-wow; she taught me to read music. But to begin with, how I dreaded those piano lessons. Standing behind me as I sat despairingly on the piano stool, Bow-wow would beat time by banging me vigorously on my back so that the notes I was trying to read on the score kept jumping into a blur. 'Go on, go on', she would cry as I stumbled haltingly through 'Rock of Ages'. 'One, two, three, four, don't stop even if you play a wrong note, keep the tempo'. I longed to tell her that I would be able to see the notes better if she stopped thumping me, but didn't dare. She was right, of course, about keeping going regardless of wrong notes and after many tearful dreaded sight-reading lessons I began to get the hang of it. Then a new world began to open for me and what, up till then had been boredom and drudgery took on a new look. I began to enjoy practising, for now a lot of the time was spent reading new things instead of going over and over my 'piece'. In a way this ability to read music well was a hindrance to memorising it, but on the other hand, I acquired the same longing to find out what was in the next 'chapter' as though I had been reading an exciting story. This encouraged me to sit and play which naturally gave me plenty of practice. Curiously, though perhaps in character, mother showed only grudging interest in my developing talent but father was thrilled to have a budding pianist in the family. Soon, he and I were tackling duets together and as my pianistic talents blossomed he would make me play to him in the evenings. For this I shall always feel grateful, though I found it rather an ordeal at the time. All the same I longed for my mother's approval. Most unnecessarily, I think, she must have felt jealous of my success such as it was, because although she was so gifted herself as a composer and a poet, she was never a pianist.

I forget how long Bow-wow reigned – quite the longest of all the dragons-in-charge. Then one day she frightened us all out of our wits when she had a stroke or a fit and flopped across the schoolroom table very red in the face and snoring loudly. Mother tried two or three more dragons, but eventually grew tired of the whole regime and sent us to a small day school in Claygate.

6

Doughty House, Richmond

⊰━━━⊱

Up to the age of fourteen, when my father's mother, Bessie Cook, died I had had four grandparents. All of them except perhaps grandmamma Cook played a large part in my life. I can't honestly say that I loved either of my grandfathers unreservedly, the Bridport one because he was something of a mystery and therefore rather frightening, the Cook one because his bluff hearty manner embarrassed me. All the same, I admit to a certain warmth of affection for him, he was so obviously fond of us all, even though his way of showing it was not to our liking. Grannie Bridport we loved very much; grandmamma Cook we never saw so often nor knew so well. She was a reserved person, keeping much to herself and spending long hours in her boudoir in Doughty House, Richmond. It was in this setting of Cook's Castle, as we used to call it, that I remember her best — a tall, substantial figure in rustling black taffeta, her neck encased in whale-bone stiffened lace, the points of which made a red spot either side of her neck. She reminded me of the wire figure, a dummy called Aunt Sophy used for fittings which stood in our box room at home. In those days every female figure supposedly had the same shape, prominent bosom, tiny pinched-in waist and swelling thighs and grandmama was a perfect replica of Aunt Sophy; she looked stuffed. Her hair was always neat and tidy, year after year, but I did not then know it was a toupée. It was of a reddish tinge with a prim little fringe to match. Poor grandmamma; I think she was shy of us for she only showed us timid affection. Possibly the trying life she undoubtedly had with grandpapa must have driven her into her shell and made her very unsure of herself. She spent her days writing letters so I have been told while downstairs the galleries rang with the shouts and laughter of grandpapa and his merry company.

I can vaguely remember her in the other Cook stronghold, 24 Hyde Park Gardens, London, where we often lunched on one of our visits to the dentist or photographer and where my sister, Rachel was born. Occasionally we went for a drive with her in the Victoria round Hyde Park, usually just ourselves, mother and Ethel Cross, grandmamma's attractive secretary. Ethel Cross was always beautifully dressed, putting us all in the shade on social occasions with her elegance and charm. The airs she gave herself always ruffled mother, though there was never any need for her to feel inferior; for when mother was properly dressed there were eyes for nobody else. Ethel spoke in a deep, rather husky voice which seemed to be irresistable to the opposite sex, for though as yet unaware of the significance of such goings on, we could not help noticing how attractive she was to men. I remember one day while driving round Hyde Park there was a lull in the conversation. In a clear voice Rachel, then about four, suddenly said, 'When is a lady not a lady?' And before anybody had time to think of a more diplomatic reply and looking triumphantly at her victim, she announced with much delight, 'When she's a little cross'.

From a very early age I found grandpapa Cook intriguing, but overwhelming, and as I grew older I felt he was rather an embarrassment. I am sure he meant to be kind and was always nice to us but we disliked his somewhat familiar manner of showing his affection. He would grab hold of us, mother as well, bounce us up and down on his knees, rubbing his tickly jowls over our faces, breathing heavily of cigar, wine and lavender water which smell I, personally, rather liked, though I hated the tickles. 'Marney,' he would call to mother, 'come here, little twopenny.' And mother, despite her obvious dislike of such proceedings would be hauled onto his knee. 'Nasty old man,' she would mutter as with rumpled red hair and hot cheeks she at last managed to struggle free. It was perhaps naughty of mother to show her dislike so clearly, though I must say it never seemed to upset Grandpapa.

It was at Doughty House, Richmond, with its big collection of Old Masters and other treasures which he had inherited from his father, Sir Francis, that we saw most of Grandpapa. But he had not inherited his father's artistic qualities, taking little interest in the pictures, nor knowing much about them. Francis, my brother, has told me grandpapa did add one picture to the collection, a vast rather ugly one, wrongly attributed to Vandyke. Most of his enthusiasm was for the lighter side of life, pretty ladies, gay company, driving his coach and four and so forth. He entered into his inheritance with zest and I am sure enjoyed playing the leading part, looking proudly at the vast array of paintings through clouds of tobacco smoke and slapping everyone on the back with loud, cheerful greetings. Grandpapa was about six feet tall with a round, prominent tummy across which his gold watch chain shone and strained. He was baldheaded, at least from the time I can remember him, with side whiskers and a small scrubby beard. His nose was a bit bulbous and red (oh, that delicious port!) and his eyes small, but twinkly. Perhaps not a very attractive picture, but nevertheless he radiated a sort of hail-fellow, well-met atmosphere. I never saw him in the sort of purple rages grandfather Bridport indulged in; he blew up mostly over trivialities but soon quietened down again. We saw him, of course, whenever we went to lunch in the warehouse (at St. Paul's Churchyard). These visits were red letter days for us with the excitement of travelling up to London in the train and taking a hansom cab to our destination. We enjoyed those cabs with the driver perched far above our heads and

the horse's tail just under our noses, so that we could tweak a
hair out quite easily. The cabby from above would shout
down 'Where to?' Having told him, he would shut his trap
door, flap the reins over his horse's back and away we would
trot. We would then shut our doors or sometimes leave them
wide open if very hot. Anyhow they met in the centre and
were low enough for us to peep over. This was all right and
most enjoyable when fine, but when it rained or was cold the
thing was shut right up and became stuffy and smelly. Cabs,
growlers and flies were all modes of transportation in my
young days, all except the hansom cab four-wheeled, like our
own brougham. Alas, I cannot truthfully say I remember the
horse-drawn buses. I am quite sure I never travelled in any.

Arrived at the Warehouse, we eventually found ourselves
among the company sitting down for lunch. Grandpapa, as
head of the firm, sat at the top of the long table in the board
room, the rest, in order of seniority or importance down each
side of the table. They all seemed to us very ancient, except
father. There was Sir George Pragnell, a handsome man with
upturned grey military moustaches, always in a smart grey
suit. He had a daughter called Vera, older than I was, whom
we used to meet on other occasions but to whom I never
spoke. I felt rather piqued to think that another Vera could
look so interesting with lovely red hair, remembering my own
rats tails. There were two cousins of father's, George Gribble
and Cecil Cotton. Another nice man was Percy Howes who
married Ethel Cross, grandmamma's attractive secretary.
Percy had a fearsome stammer and when seated next to him
at lunch my appetite completely vanished at the possibility
of being spoken to by him; but in fact, I was so engrossed in
helping him over his own difficulties that my own stammer
entirely disappeared. In all this masculine company I expect
we were pleasingly refreshing. The feast finished with port
and cigars. There was one other name among the warehouse
staff which caught my fancy and that was Venus. Mr. Venus

in later years became a valued member of the board of
directors. But all I can remember about him was the rather
poor humour we showed on the journey home by singing
with much gusto and giggles the following lines in waltz
tempo:

> Venus, Venus, we entreat you
> Come and live on earth again,
> Songs of joy we'll bring to meet you
> And a fountain of champagne.

I can't see that it even makes sense, but I suppose the vision
of Mr. Venus soaking in champagne seemed to us terribly
funny and witty.

We watched the Lord Mayor's Show many times, crowding
onto the benches in the big windows overlooking the route.
This was great fun but the walk through the departments was
less enjoyable. It seemed to me a huge place, dark and stuffy,
and full of strange shapes like grandmama and our Aunt
Sally, with enormous busts but no legs. The calico section
was quite nauseating, smelling of castor-oil, just as in Mr.
Styles' drapery shop in Esher.

A great deal of Cook, Son and Co. was destroyed by
bombs and fire during the blitzes in 1942. It has since been
rebuilt and modernised and now calls itself Cook & Watts.

A more intriguing picture comes to my mind of grandpapa,
resplendent in grey suit and topper with flower in buttonhole
driving his four-in-hand. Sometimes he drove over to Copseham, about twelve miles from Richmond to see us and to let
us see him. I well remember one unusual happening. We were
standing with my parents and a crowd of their friends on the
croquet lawn one hot afternoon waiting for him to arrive. In
the distance we could hear the thin, faint note of the coach
horn getting louder and clearer as grandpapa with his
coachload of smartness and beauty approached. The exciting
clatter of sixteen iron-clad hooves on the road sent us rushing
to the gate. There he was, coming along at a spanking pace,

really rather a thrilling sight on a quiet country road. Hardly slackening speed, grandpapa swung the team round at right angles to get through the entrance gates but, alas, a slight miscalculation brought a wheel scraping along one of the gate-posts. Everything came to a sickening stop; horses leaping up and down, ladies screaming, grandpapa shouting and swearing, and Brassington, the coachman bravely rushing into the shambles to restore order. This was regarded as a shameful occurrence and far from amusing; but to us, though, it had seemed most exciting and very, very funny. Looking at that narrow entrance as I did some years ago, I do think there was a little excuse for grandpapa; but of course he was taking it much too fast; showing off invariably ends in disaster.

When I was out of the nursery and could be trusted to behave more or less correctly I was sometimes included in the coach party. I have recently been told by a friend who was very 'horsey' in her young days, that I was wrong to call the vehicle which grandpapa drove a 'coach'; she remembers a coach was more like a wagonette with a roof, at any rate a covered conveyance and the vehicle grandpapa had should have been called a 'drag'. Perhaps a 'drag' did not sound quite so grand as a 'coach'. Many people had a coach and four in those days (surely a drag and four sounds a bit odd?), and it was a fine sight to see a gathering of these smart affairs full of elegantly dressed people, not forgetting the fine horses with shining harness and jingling bits. Hurlingham, Ranelegh and Osterly Park were the favourite meeting places and it was to these rendezvous that I went in the Cook four-in-hand in company with many similar turn-outs. Our four bright bays made as good a show as any and I felt proud of grandpapa. He drove dashingly and I think, very well, for to control four excited well-fed horses needs a good pair of hands and a steady nerve. As usual, on these occasions, he was dressed to the nines, grey topper jauntily tilted, a flower in his lapel and beside him on the box a pretty lady. It is a funny thing but I can't remember ever being on the coach with grandmamma though undoubtedly she did go as the photograph shows. This photo I guess must have been taken about 1896-7, two or three years before father was married. He stands at the back of the coach holding the coach horn, his parents on the box, his elder sister with friends on the coach and his younger sister on a magnificent tricycle. I have no idea where the photo was taken.

When I first began to be included in these outings I was much impressed by the gay joviality of the occasion. Surrounded by the usual crowd (including my bête noir, Colonel Broome) in picture hats, toppers and parasols, grandpapa was in his element and beaming with pleasure. Into this jolly mass I was squeezed, usually between grandpapa and his lady, minus picture hat and parasol but happy and excited. Brassington was the head coachman in those days and was the star of the outings. He was a big, fat man with a very red face; in his smart livery he looked a regular John Bull. Whenever I looked back from my seat on the box I could just see Brassington hanging out at a perilous angle from the back step, straining his a : to catch a glimpse of the leaders prancing away in front. When preparing to sound the horn he blew himself out like some monstrous bull-frog. His voice too was stentorian. Once as we were approaching some low-hanging branches at full speed it was only Brassington's bellow of ' 'ats, ladies, 'ats' that saved a full scale tragedy. For such a big man, he was very agile. As soon as grandpapa pulled up or any of the horses misbehaved, Brassington nipped down from behind and was at their heads in a flash, blowing like a grampus, sweat pouring down his fat, red face. Perhaps he did not have quite such a good opinion of grandpapa's capabilities as I had; anyway he was always at the business end when we came to a stop. Once, he let me drive. He was exercising the horses in Richmond Park and I was beside him on the box. Perhaps it would be more accurate to say that he allowed me to hold the reins. I was staggered by the weight of them; my arms seemed likely to burst out of their sockets as I struggled to control the four cavorting animals so far below and ahead of me, especially the leaders which didn't seem to be connected with the wheelers at all. After that experience I had a lot more sympathy for grandpapa trying to manoevre that thing round sharp bends and through gateways.

Copseham being reasonably near Doughty House meant that we drove over sometimes on Sundays to have tea with the grandparents. It seemed a terribly long drive to us sitting primly in the brougham dressed in our best. And after spending a few hours at Doughty there was the long drive home again. Occasionally we were invited to stay and went with our nursery retinue for a week or so. Our rooms were right at the top of the house with the famous view of the Terrace and the winding Thames spread out before us, for our delight. And, indeed, I loved being there, standing at those windows watching the world coming and going. With still so few cars on the roads, there was a quiet dignity about the terrace along which we bowled our wooden hoops, our nannies sitting on the seats gossipping with other nannies. Nothing worse than a harmless collision with other people's hoops out of control upset these simple outings. When we returned, we were supposed to go straight upstairs – the back stairs, of course. We were never allowed to go into the galleries by ourselves for fear we might do harm to the pictures or other treasures. In fact, we almost stopped breathing and certainly always walked on tip-toe when passing the many valuables on walls and landings. Running, of course, was strictly forbidden in case we skidded into an Old Master. It was a very awe-inspiring place for children but I am sure it did us no harm. Even though we found the restrictions and discipline somewhat burdensome they did instil into our hooligan minds some respect for beautiful things. Not that I appreciated the beauty of the paintings, some, I thought, quite hideous and some of the portraits I definitely hated and hurried passed them as quickly as I could, without running. I thought they looked at me with equal dislike as though they resented me being there. This fear did not get much less even when we moved from Copseham to live at Doughty after grandpapa died. With the best will in the world, one could never call Doughty a home; it was a Gallery and a Museum first and last and if we did not fit in as museum pieces and part of the collection that was nobody's fault but ours.

The mummy-cases in the museum below the long gallery were terrifying things. When I was very tiny I hated going down there with grandpapa because I knew he would insist, though very jovially, on me stepping inside one. He would open the painted wooden door gaily, tell me to get in, then shut the door on me. There I would wait, my heart in my mouth, holding my breath as long as possible so that I wouldn't smell the musty smell of the last occupant's body and praying that grandpapa wouldn't go away and forget I was there.

The whole museum was conducive to nightmares in a young child, though I don't remember suffering any ill effects; directly I had climbed the stairs to the gallery above I forgot about mummies and tombs, until my next visit. I never enjoyed the atmosphere of that place even when grown up. As well as mummies and tombs and alabaster baths, there were busts of Roman emperors with most unpleasant faces. There was always a peculiar smell down there, too, which for a long time I was convinced could be nothing else but the smell of rotting bodies, but which I think was mainly due to lack of fresh air and all the stale tobacco smoke. Every now and then bangs and strange noises like groans and snores reverberated through the rooms and I would take to my heels and run upstairs. I eventually realised that these noises were only the coach horses stamping and snorting in the near-by stables. Even when considerably older a chill crept down my spine when I was sent down to prepare the billiard table for a game with father. The table here was a full size one, harder for me than the three-quarter sized one I had learned on at Copseham. When I was older still and my irresponsible London friends came down for the evening we would play fives on it, officially not allowed. This joyful occupation is bad enough for the well-being of any billiard table but when Roman emperors and valuable Etruscan vases and so on stand in the line of fire the risk of damage is much more serious. We did, most considerately hang the table cloth and Persian rugs over the emperors, vases and tombs and, miraculously, no damage was done.

7

Music and Doughty

Music and Doughty are inseparable. When my great-grand-father, Sir Francis, built the galleries for his picture collection he made a room for music at the end of the long gallery beyond the octagon room. Here he put a small, but very lovely-toned, organ built by Norman Hill and Bairds. Across its frame was carved in gilded lettering 'If Music be the Food of Love – play on'. I never could quite understand the connection but I think Love must have been thoroughly over-worked. When we went to live at Doughty, as also was the Steinway grand; at one time when the great pianist George Chavchavadze was living with us there, we had a Bechstein, too.

Long before I myself can remember anything about Doughty, the Sunday afternoon gathering there had become famous. Great-grandpapa liked showing his pictures to his appreciative friends, very naturally, for what could be nicer than to stroll through the galleries among famous paintings to the accompaniment of swelling organ and indeed of music of all kinds? Things got rather out of hand in Grandpapa's day for friends invited friends and so on and grandpapa's friends were not for the most part art connoisseurs, so what had originated as an intellectual and musical delight became more like comic opera. But this was not by any means always the case because I can clearly remember long before we were actually living at Doughty that there was much wonderful music of all kinds and many wonderful performers.

Thinking about those Sunday afternoons as I often do

with nostalgia for that distinctive and unforgettable atmosphere of stale cigar and warm stuffiness, I am aware also of some slightly sinister influence creeping through the galleries. This, in time, I came to realise, from whispered insinuations and shocked expressions, was the shadow of my step great-grandmama Tennessee Claflin, whom my great-grandfather married in 1885, one year after his first wife had died. This strange character was the tenth and last child of one Reubin Claflin and his wife and was born in Ohio. I have recently read a book by Johanna Johnstone called *Mrs. Satan* which gives a most interesting account of this peculiar family and the life histories of the two famous sisters, Victoria and Tennessee. Both became the first women brokers on Wall Street and together published a very controversial journal called *Woodhull and Claflin's Weekly*. Both advocated free love for women, practised it and lectured about it. Both were clairvoyantes and it is possible that this mutual interest in Spiritualism formed a bond between Sir Francis and Tennessee. What a remarkable character she must have been, whatever one thinks of her activities! Her name was hardly ever mentioned in the family so that it was difficult for me to know of what crime she was accused. The chief complaint seemed to be that she deliberately left pamphlets and tracts about 'free love' all around the galleries, slipped into the catalogues and so on, a scandalous and contaminating habit. How I would have loved to have met her, but of course we never had the chance, though I was already a young married woman when she died in 1924. How the galleries must have sparkled when step-great-grandmamma arrived to shatter their stiff Victorian correctitude! I wonder so much about her; was she tabooed when the new Lady Cook, my grandmamma came to Doughty; and how did she get on with her step-son, my grandpapa? There seem so few, if any, records of her life with the Cook family, though I did read the following account in a newspaper cutting on the death of Sir Francis. Tennessee's great niece, Utica Welles, became engaged to a talented young musician called Thomas Beecham and this event was announced and celebrated in the garden of Doughty House. As the Beecham marriage was in 1903 and my great-grandfather died in 1901, then the engagement must have been an unusually long one or was celebrated after his death. If this latter was the case, then the Dowager Lady Cook had still the entrée of Doughty House.

During Grandpapa's life-time we often drove over from Copseham for these Sunday musicals; mother hated this because it meant having to dress in her best and help to entertain crowds of people, some complete strangers. When we were older father expected us, too, to take an active part in the proceedings by talking to the visitors about the pictures, in fact, to act as well-informed guides. I always hoped there would be so much music to listen to that nobody would worry too much about who painted what and when. Anyhow, I definitely preferred to listen to the music which was well worth listening to, for practically always there would be some celebrity to sing or play and always the organ rumbling and pulsating through the galleries. The Montague Phillips often gave a recital including some of David's own songs and extracts from his operetta *The Rebel Maid* and from *Lilac Time* in both of which Phillipa had taken the leading part in the London productions. Miller, the Richmond Church organist and later, Ambrose Porter who succeeded him there and who ultimately became organist of Lichfield Cathedral, both came to contribute towards the programmes. If all else failed, which thank goodness was very seldom, the family was called upon to fill the breach. For me, this meant accompanying the soloist, voice or instrument including mother with her concertina and playing duets for two pianos or piano and organ. Much later, after I had left school and was having piano lessons from Arthur de Greef, the Belgian pianist, I sometimes had to play a solo. This was an ordeal in any circumstances, but infinitely worse if de Greef happened to be one of the guests. Even though he was

not actually sitting in the organ room watching me, I knew
he was listening to every note from somewhere in the
galleries and that I would be sure to hear all about my
performance when I went to the Green room in the dear old
Queen's Hall for my next lesson. De Greef was a first class
teacher, by then in his seventies. Working with him was a
revelation and he made every lesson that much more
wonderful when he talked about his old friends, Brahms and
Grieg especially. He himself, sometimes played at Doughty
and listening to him playing Grieg made me feel proud of
being his pupil.

I have forgotten many of the artists who came to those
musical afternoons but I clearly remember Clara Butt and her
husband Kennerly Rumford, for apart from her magnificent
voice, Clara Butt had a charming personality and nobody
could fail to like her. When she sang 'Home Sweet Home'
sometimes just a shade off pitch to Miller's organ accompaniment, the sound came rolling down the galleries rich and full
like one of the big organ stops. I remember wallowing
sentimentally in Hubert Eisdell's sweet tenor voice singing
that delicious ditty called 'I'll sing thee Songs of Araby'
composed, if I remember rightly, by one Frederick Clay, and
in the soft brogue of Pat Byrne singing old Irish melodies.
Then there was Gervaise Elwes looking like an aristocratic
butler with a bald head singing Quilter's settings of Shake-
speare's Sonnets. And our life long Danish friend, Joe Nilson,
once the leading tenor in the Carl Rosa opera company,
whose glorious voice and splendid Viking looks made him
indeed a star turn. Once Ysaye the Belgian violinist, gave a
recital. I was fascinated to see that his fingers looked like ten
short fat bananas, not in the least what I thought they ought
to look like.

And here I must digress from recounting the events of my
early years and the memory of those musical Sundays to
write a few words about a great friend and artist who above

everyone else has left a brighter light on the scene than any other fine performer.

Prince George Chavchavadze was sent to an English school towards the end of the First World War when he was about 14. Later, when his family joined him over here from their exile in Roumania, we got to know them well and they became and remain some of our dearest friends. George was undoubtedly a child prodigy, playing Beethoven Sonatas at the age of five, going on to Mozart and Liszt and composition before his teens. When he was about seventeen my father, one of the great connoisseurs of art, having been much struck by George's musical gifts arranged for him to come and live permanently at Doughty House so that he could continue his musical studies and share the tutor, then 'finishing off' my brother Francis and a young friend, Walter Kingsbury. In such surroundings, immersed in so much beauty and culture, George's music went ahead rapidly. Whenever I think of Doughty and Monserrate (of which more anon) I naturally think of George and vice versa and all that his music meant to me and those who heard him play. And not for his music alone. George was gifted in so many ways that it is difficult to single out any one talent above others, but I think perhaps his great sense of the ridiculous was one of the strongest and most endearing of his traits. This talent enabled him to dramatise and produce the most rip-roaring, deliciously naughty solo farces so that his fascinated audience became incapable of anything but helpless laughter. To this stimulating side to his character he could add brilliance as a raconteur second to none. He excelled in dancing, swimming and tennis and with the same facility with which he triumphed as a pianist he shone as a singer of songs in almost every language, having a fine natural voice and acting ability.

As the years passed I saw less of George as we went our different ways, he to tour the country and later, Europe, I to a more hum-drum existence. He went to some of the finest teachers, of whom perhaps Miss Lander had the greatest influence on his musical development. Miss Lander was the founder and teacher of the Leschetisky School in London and a pupil of the famous old Professor. Benno Moiseivitch took a personal interest in the young virtuoso and later, with Miss Lander's approval, George went to Poland to study under Egon Petri, the most famous pupil of the Liszt-Busoni School.

The highest point of his musical career, I suppose must have been the Concert he gave in the Carnegie Hall in 1947 when Virgil Thompson, the distinguished New York music critic, proclaimed George one of the six finest pianists in the world. And in 1949 when Paris was celebrating the Chopin Centenary, George was sent for from America in order to play the music of the Master of which he was considered the finest exponent. It is impossible here to give more than a slight sketch of this great artist but having known him as a dear friend, as well as an international musician, the memory of him is entwined in so much of my life that I could hardly do less than try to show how much he meant to us all. I hope, one day, his life and work as pianist, teacher and composer will become more widely known.

George's mother, 'Moushka' to her many friends, and his step-father, Peter Troubetzkoy, settled near us in Purbeck for their remaining years. His elder brother, Paul, the author, married Princess Nina of Russia and lived at Cape Cod in the United States but to our sorrow died last year. Marina, George's sister, lives in Kent doing wonderful work in Dorothy Kerin's nursing home at Groombridge and is one of my dearest friends.

Here is an extract from a letter from Paul which perhaps conveys something of the regard which his friends and all lovers of music had for George. Paul is here quoting from a letter he had received from a lady in Washington (whom he did not know) after the news of George's death in a car crash in France had become known.

By a strange coincidence, exactly fifteen years ago today, your family and mine were, at this very moment attending a concert in Carnegie Hall where a great pianist gave an unforgettable performance of incredible virtuosity and exquisite beauty. As if it were only yesterday I remember the strains of the Waldstein Sonata with which he opened his concert. A man who has left such indelible memories in the hearts of people here and abroad and afforded so many hours of happiness will always live.

To return to the earlier days before George came into the family.

Grandpapa liked listening to music though knowing little about it. Very often, Miller, the Richmond church organist would come round in the evenings to play for him and he and later, Porter, were always there to organise the Sunday afternoon concerts. It was while Miller was playing one Sunday that Olga and I made a momentous discovery. Miller had always had an incredibly elegant figure with a slim waist line, but it was only when he donned a khaki uniform in the First World war that we saw the reason for his model shape. As he sat at the organ his arms strained forward over the manuals, we could see, much to our glee and quite distinctly, the outline of corsets. I think we had enough decency not to broadcast the news, at least not very far, though it was most tempting.

During a Sunday afternoon's performance the bulk of the visitors gathered in the organ room sitting on the old Spanish leather chairs grouped round the mosaic floor. Grandpapa sat on the red velvet seat of his carved oak arm-chair with a high back, drumming on its arms with his fingers and nodding his head in time to the music. Handel's *Largo* was his favourite piece and had to be included in every recital. He liked singing, too, especially if the singer was a pretty lady. I always hoped to escape notice when I crept in to listen, but inevitably grandpapa would see me and beckon me over to him. Then I would have to sit either on his knees or squashed in beside him on the velvet seat and try to enjoy the music interspersed with heavy breathing and loud whispers wreathed in cigar smoke, accompanied by affectionate squeezes of the ribs. To round off an exhausting but stimulating afternoon, there would be a sumptuous tea laid out in the Drawing-room with butler and footmen flying around with plates of cakes and cups of tea or iced coffee and mother, looking quite enchanting in her best and hating every minute of it perched on a satin covered chair, smiling and talking to the chattering mob.

8

Vale

◄═══════►

Before I close the door on Doughty House with all its
memories of those Sunday gatherings, I would like to go once
again as I used to, along that long, darkened length of gallery
to the Organ room for my daily practice. From quite an early
age, whenever we were staying at Doughty on a visit I was
supposed to do my piano practise daily. Strangely, this ordeal
always seemed to be scheduled for the evening, after tea,
when the sombre, stuffy galleries, silent and empty yet
horribly alive, seemed to stretch into infinity with the Organ
room out of sight and, to me almost unattainable.

The parallel double galleries were built onto the first,
original gallery at right angles, converging into the octagon
room and finishing in the organ room. Over all this stretched
the double glass roof in which was the enormous array of
electric light bulbs needed to light the place.

With sinking heart, I leave the warm, bright lived-in part of
the house and creeping through the first gallery soon find
myself standing on the steps leading into the right side of the
double gallery, usually called the Long Gallery. On my left,
on a gilded chest stands 'The Three Marys' by Van Eyke, the
treasure of the collection. This picture, after hair-raising
escapades during World War Two when for some time it was
'lost' on the Continent finished up safely in Holland in the
Van Beunigan collection in Rotterdam where it is now.

I draw aside the two heavy bead-embroidered velvet
curtains and stand for a second peering into darkness. On my

right is the switch board, a massive affair with umpteen switches. At the bottom of this panel on the right is the one and only switch I am allowed to touch. I turn it down, resisting the urge to run my hands over the whole lot. Far away in the distance a soft, muted light appears, shining through an alabaster bowl on a stand. This 'night-light' effect is all I am allowed to have to guide me on my way; I therefore begin my walk in semi-darkness. I can feel eyes following my every step; arms with groping fingers reach for me. Run! Run! Faster! Faster! My feet fly over the persian rugs in a panic rush and strictly forbidden till, at the end of the gallery I suddenly find myself confronted by the Apollo Belvedere, a deadly white, more than life-size figure, and looking, if possible, more gigantic than ever in the pale glow from the alabaster bowl. Opposite him, but not directly in my path, stands Venus, another huge shape gazing towards him and clutching inadequate draperies around her pallid form. But I am not interested in their problems, to me they simply represent the end of the longest and possibly the worst part of my journey. But there are still plenty of hurdles ahead, I know, so I plunge into the cold darkness of the octagon room knowing that my goal, the organ room, lies beyond that again. The pale light throws a faint glow over some dark, enormous shape in front of me that seems to be filling the entire room. I stretch out my hands and touch the ice-cold side of a huge, dark red, porphry bowl. Round this thing I sidle clinging to its chilly surface more from necessity than affection, till instinct warns me I must be opposite the entrance to the organ room. I dart across the last few feet of floor and to boost up my courage run my hands rapidly over the switch board by the door (again strictly forbidden) and for a moment or two stand in brilliance. I really don't know which is worse, imagining the things on the walls or seeing them suddenly startlingly alive and all around me.

There is a curious atmosphere about the organ room difficult to define but it seems to me more hostile than any of the galleries except maybe for the museum below. Perhaps it is that here nearly all the pictures are painted by Spanish artists with that touch of cold cruelty which is lacking in the warmer Dutch and Italian paintings. High up and in the corner beyond the piano I can see a large hole in one of the pictures entirely obliterating the face of one of the figures. This painting, by Gallegos, is one of twentyfive panels covering the entire east wall of the room and had once formed part of the altar piece in the cathedral of Ciudad Rodrigo. During the Peninsular War a cannon ball had removed Judas Iscariot's head. The hole was never repaired. Another series of panels shows scenes from the Day of Judgement, one of which consists of hundreds of naked bodies tumbling out of tombs and sepulchres. To take the taste out of my mouth I look with relief at Velasquez's painting called 'The Omelette' which now hangs in the Edinburgh collection. One of my favourites hangs near by, another Velasquez, painted when he was a young man at the Spanish Court. It is called the 'Calabacillus' and shows a full length portrait of the Court Fool in a black tunic. His pale, gentle face stares vacantly at us; no hostility here, only sadness; one wonders what kind of a life the Spanish Court had given him. This wonderful painting now hangs in an American gallery. Quite a contrast is the picture hanging on the left of the entrance, at eye level and in my opinion the nicest, or perhaps the second nicest in the room. This is the portrait of 'A Young Cavalier' by Rizzi. I feel drawn to this boy because his round, red cheeks and straight rat's tails are like mine; even the family have noticed the likeness. He stands with one podgy hand resting on the table, clad in a yellow satin coat with lace collar and cuffs, brown velvet breeches, short leather boots with spurs on his feet and a sword buckled round his waist. I once went to a village hall fancy dress dance many years later as an exact replica of this picture, but it rather missed the point because few, if any, of the worthy village folk had ever seen the picture. 'A Young

Cavalier' now hangs in my brother's collection in his home in Jersey.

The picture hanging above the Rizzi is quite the nastiest there, in my opinion. It is Valdes Leal's painting of St. Bonaventura, after death, writing his memoirs of St. Francis. There he sits, pen in hand, his clay coloured face and sunken cheeks realistically corpse-like. I rather think he wears a tricorn hat, why I couldn't say, perhaps my memory has let me down. Two more pictures catch my eye, the doll-like figure of a young Infanta and the nicest one in the room 'The Old Beggar Man' by Michelin. This old chap, holding a bottle of wine and dressed in a mass of rags, has such a merry, smiling face so creased in wrinkles that there is barely an inch of smooth skin to be seen. I always felt that in spite of his being quite an old rascal I wouldn't have minded being in the room alone with him, which is more than I can say about the others.

I now have to switch off all the lights except the two standing on the piano and with this august company staring at me, I clatter noisily across the mosaic floor. Unless one wears rubbers, which were unusual in those days, it is impossible to walk quietly on such a floor and in that silent room every sound seems magnified a thousand fold. I am just plucking up courage to shatter the silence with my first notes when a curious noise sends my heart into my mouth and I glance uneasily over my shoulder at the organ. Like a giant having a bad dream, the bellows are slightly puffing and wheezing. This sometimes happened if the organ had been recently played and turned off. Then silence. Again I turn to the piano and this time I get going and am beginning to enjoy myself when — Oh, heavens, what can that be? Muffled bangs reverberate from below and in imagination I see naked bodies bursting open sepulchres and mummy-cases. Of course, I know exactly what makes the tiresome noises because they continue on and off for most of my practice hour; but even knowing the culprits are only the coach horses stamping and snorting in the stables below doesn't really make them any less suggestive.

After a while, the lovely sound (yes, even scales and exercises sound ravishing in those accoustics) from a lovely instrument in the midst of such a company, seen and unseen, outweigh all else and I play and play, sometimes beyond the allotted time. Before setting off on the return journey, I cannot resist the temptation to try the organ. This pleasure is not forbidden provided everything is left as it should be and, of course, the organ turned off. I switch it on and the bellows inflate with huge, bronchial inhalations. Quickly, I pull out all the biggest stops and the galleries are flooded with a burst of sound. Up to the time when I had lessons on the Esher Church organ from Montague Phillips my playing had been 'by guess and by God', most satisfying to me and certainly impressive, from a distance.

After that explosion, I moderate my ardour and reluctantly decide to call it a day. I turn off the organ and tidy the music sheets. Except for the usual gasps from the expiring bellows, the silence that now engulfs me seems louder than ever.

Then begins the long trek back to civilisation, the same procedure but in reverse, finishing by the switch board and the Van Eyke. I must never forget to turn off the alabaster light which, after such a scurrying retreat I might easily do. This lovely little Organ was dismantled at the beginning of the 1939 War which it spent in safety in a Methodist chapel in South Wales. After the War, it was moved to the Methodist Church in Love Street (most appropriately) at Paisley, Scotland.

Grandpapa died, after a long illness, in May 1920, just before my coming-out dance at the Ritz. This, of course, had to be cancelled, to my great disappointment. Not so to mother. Hating such social functions, she was obviously much relieved and, I think, for once felt grateful to grandpapa. He lay in state in front of the organ, the floor smothered in flowers and to the strains of his much-loved Handel's *Largo* he was carried away through the galleries to his final resting place in Richmond cemetery.

9
Friends

———

I would not like to give the impression that we did not enjoy meeting the people who filled the galleries those Sunday afternoons; of course we did and knew many of them well. To be quite honest though, there were some we could have done without. Most of them were our parents' friends, some even of grandpapa's vintage and some just plainly gate-crashers.

Reviewing the scene as I now can do, from a distance, I would say that, while father loved to bask in the bright lights of old families, titles and intellectual giants, mother was almost supremely indifferent to such things; she was happier with people in humbler walks of life. Father struggled, largely unsuccessfully because of mother's stubbornness, to establish liaisons with the cultured and influential both for himself and us. Mother, shying away from anything she thought savoured even remotely of snobbism went to the opposite extreme; she suspected anyone coming from the top drawer as being inevitably conventional, stupid and boring (bar herself) and was convinced that the down-trodden lower strata was oozing genius and originality, if only given the chance to show it.

The truth is that mother herself was something of a genius with her gifts of music and poetry and I can well understand and sympathise with her dislike of the conventionalities of social life when they camouflaged, as they so often did, the non-existence of anything of value.

Father had a fine well-disciplined intellect, untouched by

genius and hampered by an excessively emotional nature. He adored being adored and flattered though he recognised flattery for what it was worth, as a rule. No one knew better than he how often great wealth can be a barrier to sincere friendship but in these matters, especially where fair ladies were concerned, his heart was inclined to get the upper hand.

Mother, too, loved being admired and flattered without being as discerning as father, swallowing everything handed out to her, hook, line and sinker. Even when we were very young we could see something obvious and nauseating about some of the people who swarmed and fawned about them. But far outnumbering all these were the hosts of good and faithful friends who travelled with them through life, many of whom are still living and hold warm memories of them in their hearts. I like to remember these good friends; first and foremost of course they were our parent's friends who because of the love and esteem they had for each other became, many of them, valued friends of mine.

I suppose the closest friend of both over the years was Marjorie Johnson. She was called Wag by everybody but I am not really sure why. She had been to the same school in Bognor as mother and had eventually married Oswald Carnegie Johnson, a Balliol friend of father's. I cannot remember a time without Wag, she seemed to be always around but we never felt she was an intruder; this was more so after her marriage broke up. Oswald ('my late departed') according to Wag, we never saw again.

If mother had to be away Wag was always asked to take charge. She was a colourful and original person with many talents; in her company one was never bored. In appearance not unlike an intelligent bird with a small head of fine untidy hair, a beak-like nose and a rather receding chin. As her deafness increased over the years, her temper became more peppery, she blew up over trifles turning a violent turkey cock red all over her face and neck. Poor Wag, I think she must have found life difficult at times with both father and (*top*) The Organ room at Doughty; the setting for the Sunday afternoon musical parties. (*centre*) The Smoking-room at Doughty. At the far end on the left stands the van Eyck, with the large tondo by Fra Fillipo Lippi on the end wall. (*bottom*) The Long Gallery, leading to Octagon and Organ rooms with the statues of Apollo and Diana at the far end. On the right the collection of Dutch paintings

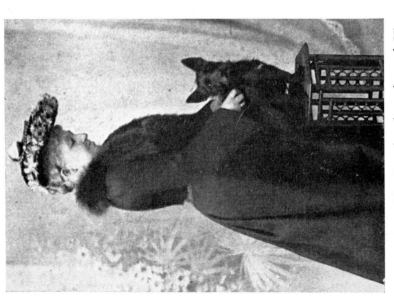

My Grandmother, the 2nd Viscountess Bridport, and Sir Francis Cook, 1st Bart, founder of the Doughty House Art Collection, creator of Monserrate and the Botanical Gardens

mother, neither of whom were very tolerant of people who irritated them, often through no fault of their own. And Wag's deafness was certainly most trying, particularly when she insisted she was *not* deaf. For instance, father, at mealtimes would say something to her, deliberately sotto voce which even we could barely hear. Naturally, no response, Wag went on eating her food. Looking indignantly round the table, eyes on the end of stalks, father would repeat his remark a little more loudly, then fortissimo. Whereupon Wag, looking very surprised at father's angry face and popping eyes would say, in the quiet voice of the deaf 'My dear Herbert, you needn't shout at me, I can hear perfectly well if you speak in your ordinary voice'.

Wag was my champion, never afraid to speak her mind to mother when she considered I had been unfairly treated. Many were the times I was rescued from a tight corner by her thoughtful kindness. I am thankful I was able to see her almost up to the time of her death from cancer when she was at Marnhull and we at Childe Okeford during the last war. This was about a year after mother died, so it must have been in 1944. I remember when I broke the news to Wag of mother's death she exclaimed in great distress 'Oh, why could it not have been me, she was younger than me and had so much to live for'. Like old familiar friends devotedly attached to each other, she and mother had many a quarrel. Mother, who smoked too much herself was forever scolding Wag for her incessant chain smoking and for the nasty smoker's cough which was the result. That, and her tea drinking and, later, a succession of yapping and snapping Yorkshire terriers, combined to irritate us all. Nevertheless, I can see now, looking back, how much my parents valued her and how good they were to her; and how much she loved them and us.

It is impossible to write of all the many friends who came to stay at Copseham, Doughty House, Monserrate and Studland. For mother, a procession of admirers. She was an enchanting

creature with her dark red hair, very blue eyes and sparkling
vitality. Music certainly was the basis of many of these
friendships. The German tenor, von Varlich came to sing and
one day he brought with him an American friend called
Chester Fentress, who besides being a singer himself with a
fine tenor voice, became mother's devoted and adoring slave
and our much loved friend. Hennie, as we called him, was
kind and avuncular and teased and ragged us incessantly. We
all adored him. He gave me on my marriage a fine cabochon
emerald ring which had once belonged to an Eastern
potentate and a similar ruby one to Rachel. During the war,
Hennie remained in New York. Mother's death in 1943
affected him deeply and he himself died a few years later. I
think probably Wag and Hennie meant more to us than any
of the many other delightful people we came to know so
well.

The fascinating, good-looking and eccentric Tollemache
family came in shoals to stay. Their kinsman was old Lord
Dysart who lived in beautiful, historic Ham House, not very
far from Doughty. We very often used to drive there from
Doughty to the afternoon gatherings. He was blind and when
I remember him was also getting very deaf. He used to be
pushed about in a wheel chair among his guests. Poor old
man, he did not enjoy those social afternoons very much and
he found it very trying having to wait for everybody to leave.
We must have been some of the last to go on the Sunday I am
thinking about because I can remember people going up to
his chair to shake hands with him and his obvious irritation as
the ceremony went on and on, till at last he could bear no
more and shouted in a thin, quavering voice 'Oh, why don't
they go, why don't they go'. I must say I sympathised with
him. I forget how many Tollemaches there were, but the
branch of the family we knew so well was seemingly endless
as were their christian names. Thirteen was the least number
anyone had and every member could include in his or her list
the name Leo and all derivatives therefrom, and finishing

with Plantaganet Tollemache. For instance, the four lovely sisters whom we knew as 'pseudo' aunts were Lyona, Lyoness, Lyonetta and Lyonella and the youngest brother, Lyonulph. Lyoness, fair haired and blue eyed, married Frank Astley-Cooper and their daughter, Theodora, became a great friend of Olga's and mine. When we were schoolgirls we would spend many weeks of the holidays with the Astley-Coopers in their cottage at Hemingford Abbots, Huntingdon, and what fun we had riding bareback over the countryside and fishing for eels at dusk in the punt on the river. How many joyous hours we spent in the little cupboard under the stairs developing our photographic efforts. How envious I was of Theo because she had plates and I only films! We saw more of the youngest sister, Lyonetta or Valentine as she was always called, than of the others. Anyhow she was the last to get married and so stayed more often at Copseham. On one of these visits I, for some reason, possibly because of a cold, was sleeping in the dressing room next to the spare-room which Aunt Valentine occupied. I lay in bed one morning listening with idle curiosity to the murmur of voices from her room where the housemaid was preparing her bath. Although we did have a bathroom I suppose the hip bath was pressed into service when the house was full. Soon I heard the door close on the departing maid, then the sound of splashing. I was out of bed in a second, my eye glued to the key-hole and was delighted when I beheld the red head of my pseudo aunt emerging from the steam. With intermittent glimpses of white arms, white knees and white bosoms, in fact all the rest of her when she stepped out onto the mat, I felt deliciously guilty of having seen what I should not have seen. Needless to say, I never dreamt of telling anyone of my discoveries but I regarded my unsuspecting aunt with renewed interest when next we met.

When Valentine married Paul Oppé in April 1908, Rachel and I were her bridesmaids; Rachel being just five and I just nine. The wedding was at Esher Church with our friend

Montague Phillips as organist. I have no very accurate picture in my mind of our dresses except that they were long and Kate Greenaway style, but I do remember we had flower wreaths on our heads and carried long handled baskets piled with violets and primroses. During the signing of the register we were left standing forlornly in the choir. Suddenly, to our astonishment, two small boys leapt out of the congregation and dashing up to us planted a smacking kiss on our cheeks. They retired as rapidly as they had appeared, leaving us and themselves overwhelmed with embarrassment. The one who had kissed me buried his face in his mother's lap when he got back to the pew and burst into tears. It must have been a truly horrible experience for them; I wonder if they remember it. They were the Rector's children, Dick and Martin Floyer. It seemed to amuse everybody but ourselves.

Apart from 'communal' friends of both parents and ourselves, father and mother had their own more personal friends. Father being much involved in the world of art was constantly writing to and meeting other connoisseurs like himself, some of whom would come to stay at Copseham from time to time, though not always becoming 'buddies' of ours. In fact we held such people as Bernard Berenson, Lord Duveen, Dr. Tancred Borenius and others somewhat in awe, and rightly so. The Witt family however, became very frequent and welcome visitors possibly because their son (now Sir John, Director of the National Gallery) was the same age as my brother, Francis. Once a very colourful sounding person came to stay, Mr. Everard Green, the Rouge Dragon. I was prepared to be quite frightened, visualising a large green dragon with a red tail and was disappointed to meet just a cheerful, plump man with an embarrassing stutter.

Some of mother's rather special friends were the Schillers who lived in Esher; three distinguished bachelor brothers who lived there with their old mother and were responsible for inspiring mother with her love for mountaineering. With them she went sometimes to Switzerland to climb the Alpine peaks. Max Schiller, K.C., round, smiling and bald-headed was Rachel's godfather and Ferdinand, known as Cat's Meat, darkly satanic-looking, was Francis's. But we never loved them as we did Wag and Hennie. At least, I didn't. Perhaps because neither of them was my godfather.

Members of the respective families came to stay now and then. We adored having Grannie Bridport, Aunt Sybil and Uncle Maurice. Father's parents never came. I suppose because they lived so close by, in Richmond. Anyhow, I am sure mother never went out of her way to try to persuade them to come. Sometimes father's sisters and families visited us. Mabel McCormick, his elder sister was also my god-mother. She referred to herself as Auntie Motin for some reason and for another one, even more obtuse, called both mother and me by the same name! She was tall, good looking and rather quiet with a deep voice. She played the violin very well, though I never heard her. Aunt Edie was also tall but not at all quiet. She chattered brightly about nothing much and was also musical, playing the harp, which ponderous instrument she carted around with her with considerable difficulty I should imagine, especially on hansom cabs. She was married to the Rev. Percival Pott, son of the Archdeacon, and at the time this event was too much for my father's sense of the ridiculous; 'The Cook has gone to the Pott,' he had said with twinkling eyes when the engagement was announced. Uncle Per was my much loved godfather, although until I was able to read his name I am afraid I could never hear it without the faint doubt entering my mind that he might be a kind of pussy cat with a super purr. Anything less like a pussy cat would be hard to imagine for Uncle Per was tall and spare with a thin, ascetic, beautiful face with wonderfully kind deepset eyes. We saw more of our Pott cousins than the McCormicks because they were more of our ages and also because poor Ian and Margaret McCormick were of retarded development and I regret to say we found them very trying.

Another lot of cousins, or rather second cousins, were the Ilchesters, and we sometimes went to parties at Holland House. Cousin Stavvy, the sixth Lord Ilchester, was mother's first cousin and a Trustee of the National Portrait Gallery and of the British Museum, sharing with father his interest in and knowledge of the arts. His wife was cousin Birdie; his children, Harry, Mary and John, now all dead, were more Rachel's age than mine. I remember one party particularly well because we were entertained in the gardens by a troupe of performing dogs and my delight watching the antics of many dogs of high and low degree, in particular a fat, cream coloured pug with a frilly collar round his bulging neck, stepping over the lawn very daintily on his hind legs. Aunt May — or rather my Great Aunt May — the Dowager Countess of Ilchester, was one of the most beautiful women of her time and indeed of any other. Tall, with great dark eyes and lovely dark hair, she walked like a queen and radiated dignity and charm. Even when very young, I realised that here was someone very special and admired her enormously. When I was in my teens and a budding pianist, father took me several times to tea with her and to play, rather nervously on the lovely piano in the drawing room. How kind she was to me, a shy young girl.

It was at Holland House and indeed in that very room that my parents had first met each other. Father was never tired of telling us the story. Mother was then staying with her uncle and aunt and father, an eligible young bachelor, had been invited to join the dinner party one evening. Arriving before the other guests and finding himself alone in the drawing-room, father sat down at the piano and began to play. Hearing the door open, he looked up and saw the slight figure of a young girl in a white dress and with a mass of glorious red hair standing watching him shyly. As he always said, 'And that was that.'

IO

Sudley Lodge, Bognor

The memories I have of Sudley Lodge, the Bridport's Bognor home seem, on the whole, more vivid and certainly happier ones than I have of Doughty House, the Cook's home. In spite of the fact that as far back as I can remember, which must have been when I was about two, neither Bridport grandparent was on speaking terms with the other or only barely, there seems to have been a more affectionate atmosphere and certainly a more natural one as far as we were concerned. For this grannie was responsible. We loved her dearly and she, aunt Sybil and uncle Maurice all contributed in their various ways to make us feel loved and wanted. The only fly (a very small one) in the jam was grandfather, a mysterious character whom we hardly ever saw except at lunch time when we all met in the dining room. Then he would stump into the room, bang the door crossly, tuck his table-napkin vigorously under his chin, mutter uncomplimentary remarks about the food into his ginger moustaches, shoot an occasional biting few words at grannie and stalk out again to vanish into his den.

I never worried why he and grannie met only at meal times nor why he and grannie lived in different parts of the house. I accepted this state of affairs as children do and only realised much later what lonely lives they must have led. For all the infrequency of his appearances grandfather did cast a shadow over the place which in all other respects was a haven of delights for me. And this was all due to the character of our lovable grandmother. Of course I never had an inkling that all was not well and to this day I am not sure what lead to the ultimate breakup of the family. I learnt more about grandfather as I grew older and realised he must have been a fine soldier in his day. He was appointed Captain of the 25th Regiment of Foot in 1862 and Colonel Commandant of the Somerset Regiment of Yeomanry Cavalry in 1872, the same year that he married grannie, then Lady Maria Georgiana Julia Fox-Strangeways, sister of the fifth Earl of Ilchester. He must have been an alarming commanding officer with his red hair, temper and language but a very efficient one because he was given a C.B. in 1892. He succeeded his father as second Viscount Bridport in 1904 when my old great-grandfather died at the age of 90. General Sir Alexander Bridport, the first Viscount was the only son of Nelson's niece Lady Charlotte Nelson who had married Samuel Hood. She died in 1873, the same year that my mother was born. Here was a link with the past, for mother could say that as a baby she had been held in the arms of Admiral Lord Nelson's niece, her great-grandmother.

I am sure grandfather was a difficult person to live with if the rumours about his behaviour were true. In his early married life Lillie Langtry, the 'Jersey Lily' had caught his roving eye and had held it for quite some time. Later, the same roving eye had dwelt lovingly upon the countenance of his children's French governess. By her, he had twins, so I have been told. When I first came upon the stage the strained relationship was in full swing. Mother, of course, was no longer in the family circle and had left her sister, Sybil, and her brother, Maurice, to support poor grannie. We were sublimely unconscious of the situation. Always there was a warm welcome awaiting us.

The white Georgian house stood well back from the road at the end of a long drive beneath an avenue of elms full of cawing rooks. The drive was covered with round, smooth pebbles which slipped and scrunched beneath our feet.

While our hearts beat fast with excitement, the old station 'fly' crawled slowly up the drive, for the impecunious Bridports had no carriage of their own to meet us at the station. There they would be, without fail waiting on the front door steps, grannie, aunt Sybil and uncle Maurice; never grandfather. But we couldn't care less even if we had thought about it, which we never did.

The two rooms we were given for our nurseries were on the first floor, just across the landing from grannie's room. How clearly can I still see the white enamel cot I slept in. It had clover-shaped holes punched all over top and bottom ends and sides, for air, I presume, and into these holes I would poke my small fingers. The cot had a strong painty smell which never seemed to get less over the years. I had my bath in a brown hip-bath carried into the nursery by a housemaid under the direction of grannie's housekeeper, Beeching, who had a little moustache and was a bit of a 'grenadier', according to Nannie. A big brass can of hot water and a brown enamel can of cold was also heaved in. How I enjoyed my bath in front of the big fire with the fireguard adorned with my night attire. To complete my happiness aunt Sybil and uncle Maurice finished off the proceedings by trickling cold water down my back from my toy watering can. Every morning when dressed I went across to grannie's room to say good morning. She was still in bed and so her maid Andy (who after grannie's death looked after mother devotedly till mother died) lifted me up to kiss grannie's soft scented cheek. Then away down a short flight of steps to aunt Sybil's room. This I found a very exciting place, as different from grannie's room as a farmyard from a garden of roses. Not that it was quite so niffy, but it certainly did have a good old doggy smell, as well it might, for aunt Sybil lay in bed surrounded by dogs of all sorts in baskets, on chairs and on the bed; mostly West Highlanders which she later bred for showing. I stayed there playing with the dogs and examining the countless ornaments, photos and knick-knacks that filled the shelves to overflowing, till the housemaid staggered in with bath and watercans and I departed to my breakfast.

Later, I met my aunt again in the garden and was allowed to help sweep up the leaves from the lawn. I had a wicker doll's pram into which I crammed what I could. Then, as a reward for my efforts, aunt Sybil would pack me in the pram on top of the leaves and rush me rapidly up and down the paths. In spite of a long skirt, tight waistband and a stiff collar, my aunt was remarkably athletic. Later, she became a county hockey player for Sussex which in those days must have seemed rather overdoing things and I believe was frowned upon by the family. How different from her sister, my mother, who avoided all games except croquet which she was forced to play on social occasions. But mother was one up on her sister when in later years she took to climbing the Alps, which activity never inspired aunt Sybil.

With my young aunt and uncle I was blissfully happy. Uncle Maurice carried me around on his shoulders calling me Mother Bunch and Apple-cheeks. Children were much over-dressed in those days and I was no exception in my stiff and starched frocks, petticoats and pinafores. Bare feet and sun-bathing were unheard of joys. What did it matter anyway if I did get crumpled and dirty? There was always a nannie to wash, iron and clean me.

Uncle Maurice was away a lot, being in the Navy. When playing polo somewhere abroad he was kicked on the head and had to have a trepanning operation. This meant goodbye to his naval career. When I was about eight he married Eileen Kendal and their daughter, Mollie, was born the following year. Peter, his only son, was born a year later in 1911. Three years later came the first World War and in 1915 Uncle Maurice, who in spite of his disabilities had managed to get himself into the Royal Naval Division, was reported missing, presumed killed in the Gallipoli landings. So there were left his young widow and her two children of four and five. We, as the older cousins, saw much of the little ones and although

I myself was by then almost totally involved in boarding school life, Francis, my brother, was only two years older than Mollie. Peter, following in the family tradition went to Dartmouth and into the Navy. He became third Viscount on the death of our grandfather in 1924. To our sorrow he died in July 1969, very suddenly of a heart attack on his estate in Bronte, Sicily. His young son, Alexander, is now the fourth Viscount.

But to return to Sudley Lodge. By the time uncle Maurice got married, it may even have been before, the family had split up and soon the old house was sold. Poor grannie, the shock of her son's death, added to the strain of her long unhappy matrimonial life became too heavy a burden for her to carry much longer. By degrees she became more and more senile and childish, mercifully forgetful of the sadnesses of her life.

As I remember her, grannie was always the same gentle, wonderfully kind person, never raising her voice to scold me or showing irritation over my misdeeds. She smelt like a hot house of violets and I loved to sit on her lap, her arm around me listening to her reading a story. This treat came after tea when I went down to her drawing room which was stacked with photos and paintings and all the knick-knacks of a typical Victorian room, something of a collector's paradise in these days. 'Gawd', she would say in her soft, rather bronchial voice 'Gawd is always near you and loves you, so you must try never to do anything which you know He wouldn't like'. Our readings were very often biblical and our stories strong in virtue. Dear grannie never lost an opportunity to try to raise my religious and moral standards; she exuded religious aromas along with her violets and hyacinths with which I always associate her. She adored her garden, tending her flowers with maternal solicitude. One day, after a heavy rain storm and high winds, I was standing beside her in the drawing room looking out of the Regency window with the two little doors beneath, which opened onto a flight of steps with the hyacinth beds either side. 'Come', she said, 'we must go out and see if any harm has come to my darling flowers,' and we opened the doors and stepped out. A fearful sight met our eyes. The beds filled with her lovely hyacinths looked like a battle-field, smashed bodies lying heaped in mangled abandon. Grannie gave a cry of distress and together we set to work to repair the damage as far as we could by propping the poor things up on sticks.

I don't know for certain what grannie did beside gardening and running the house and avoiding grandfather, but I think, like others in her position, she did a lot of social work in the neighbourhood.

So passed those happy days in that much loved house and garden.

The pungent smell of hot box and the scent of violets always take me back to that old walled kitchen garden with its little cinder paths along which we used to run. The cawing of rooks in the elms, the scrunch of white pebbles beneath our eager feet, the white gulls wheeling and mewing in the blue sky over the house, the smell of hyacinth and cigar, all are woven into the tapestry of that garden of Eden. No Eden I suppose is exempt from a serpent. Poor grandfather; I see I have already called him a fly in the jam and now I call him a serpent, which strictly speaking is quite inaccurate because he never harmed us nor interfered with our enjoyment in any way; in fact, he contributed quite unknowingly to each day's excitement, keeping us poised in anticipation of an un- expected meeting somewhere or other . . . There is no getting away though from the fact that his somewhat alarming presence made itself felt. For example, the smell of that cigar was the first thing one noticed inside the house. It was at its weakest in grannie's drawing room and bedroom as might be expected. We could get a pretty accurate idea, according to the strength of the smell whether he had just come in or been out some time. We used to sniff along the passage which led to his den like bloodhounds on the track.

Grandfather was a apoplectic-looking old man seemingly always on the point of eruption as the almost incessant rumblings and grumblings and hissings into his ginger moustaches seemed to indicate. He usually wore a loud brown check knicker-bocker suit with a Norfolk jacket. His hair, once a fiery red, was, when I first remember him, a rather unattractive shade of sandy brown, as likewise were his military moustaches which curled up on each cheek in an almost perfect semi-circle. Most of this facial adornment was dyed a dark brown where it had dipped into his coffee. We used to watch this performance with fascinated interest. Burying his face in the depths of his outsize cup, grandfather would take a long, noisy drink, surfacing at last with moustaches brown and dripping, looking just like a walrus. Then with his underlip he sucked in the over-hanging bits of hair on his top lip with loud squelchy sounds finishing off with a vigorous polishing up with his table napkin. We considered this very bad manners but were careful not to be caught watching him. He sat opposite grannie but hardly ever looked at her. If he did say something to her it was in such an acrid tone of voice that it made us feel embarrassed and sorry for her. Occasionally he would fix us with his hot blue eye, blow through his moustaches and dart a question at us with military precision, often not waiting for a reply if we were a bit slow in the uptake. This was about the only time he seemed to realise we were there.

We knew grandfather lived and slept in one big room on the ground floor which could once have been a billiard room. I was never invited to go there but once, greatly daring I crept along the passage and pushed open the door, which was ajar. I had just seen grandfather striding down the drive, otherwise I would never have dared to do this. A quick glance round was enough to confirm my suspicions that grandfather was indeed a sorceror or a kind of family monster kept apart as much as possible from the rest of the family, as whispered hints from the maids suggested. The walls of the room were covered with the stuffed heads of all kinds of animals, there were weapons of all sorts and sizes, racks of queer-shaped pipes and some peculiar looking instruments. I did not then know that these were the French horns he loved to play. I came to realise, later on, that the strang bellowings I could hear on and off in the distance was grandfather practising the horn and not the roaring of a family monster.

I wish I could have known him better but I was very young in the Sudley Lodge days and the family had split up by the time I might have been better able to appreciate him. I did see something of him at the end of the First War when we had a house in Upper Berkeley Street and grandfather was staying at his London Club. One evening he invited himself round to see us and brought the famous horn with the idea of getting me to play his accompaniments. I was agreeably surprised at the high standard of his playing but from the corner of my eye watched, with a certain amount of apprehension, the veins knotting and swelling in his temples and his face getting more and more purple. But all went well and feeling pleased with his success and, I hope, with my efforts, asked me to walk a little way back to his club with him. I little knew what I had let myself in for.

To get him safely across the confusion of the Marble Arch merry-go-round was my unenviable task. Grandfather's method was simple. With an imperious wave of his stick at the traffic roaring by he waited for nothing and nobody but at once stepped off the pavement into the hurly-burly, forcing buses and taxis to screeching halts. Muttering scathing remarks about the damn fools who had no business to be driving, etc. etc. and bringing blushes of embarrassment to my already heated cheeks, we somehow or other arrived unsquashed on the other side. Had I not been so concerned in getting him across I know I would have much enjoyed the colourful remarks of the enraged drivers.

The only time I can remember hearing grandfather laugh heartily was once when he was staying at Copseham and I was summoned from the schoolroom to see him in the garden where he was sitting with mother. I must have been about eleven. The craze with us at that period was developing and printing our Box Brownie camera films. Without waiting to change my overall which was stinking of hypo, I presented myself before my august grandparent. Impaling me with his piercing blue eyes, he naturally demanded to know what I had been doing. To which I quite naturally and truthfully replied that I had been developing in the schoolroom. Whereupon he burst out laughing to my intense astonishment.

Grannie, after many years of bedridden senility but happy with her musical box and other treasures from the past arranged around her bed, died peacefully in 1922. Grandfather continued to lived in Guernsey looked after by a devoted housekeeper and died there in 1924.

Monserrate as seen from the road to Cintra set in rolling countryside
with the Atlantic coastline in the distance

The white Carrara foun-
tain in its marble basin
beneath the central dome
of the palacio. The
octagonal gallery sur-
rounding the hall is of
Delhi alabaster with
trellis work design

George Chavchavadze

Captain Julian Gribble V.C., 1917

II

Monserrate - Portugal

◆━━━◆

What memories that name brings back! Visual memories and intoxicating smells; the hot scented air of a garden langorous beneath the fierce sun of an August afternoon. I see myself, a girl of thirteen lying in the shade of a blue-gum eucalyptus tree, listening drowsily to the splash and crash of the waterfall cascading from ledge to ledge in its descent from the lakes below the Serra. No other sound breaks the silence for this is siesta hour when everybody will be stretched out somewhere in the shade or on their beds after one of the enormous, delicious meals devised for us by our Portuguese cook.

The name 'Monserrate' is an 'Open Sesame' to me. The curtains of time roll apart and immediately I am in that Garden of Eden in the shade of gnarled arbutos trees, their round berries a brilliant red against the hot blue sky. I see again the bright camellias and the white trumpet flowers of the daturas dangling above the little paths winding their ways through the garden and hear the delicious sound of water dropping into stone tanks and basins in dark, ferny follies and temples. I see the long stretch of lawn descending steeply from the south-west terrace below the *palacio* down to the lily ponds, whereon somnolent swans serenely float; and on the far bank, in all its grandeur the huge trunk of a splendid eucalyptus tree rising some seventy feet to its lowest branches. 'These lawns are one of the glories of Monserrate as they are the only permanent lawns in the country and have existed since they were sown some sixty or more years ago'. Here I am quoting from an article written in August 1929 for the *Gardener's Chronicle* by Walter Oates, the then head gardener of Monserrate. Walter Oates had previously been head gardener in the Hanburys' great garden at La Mortola, Italy.

By a series of water channels all over these lawns and, in fact, throughout all the gardens, the grass retained much of its greenness during even the hottest months. Elsewhere everything lay brown and parched and as the sun rose higher so would the leaves droop lower. It seemed as though Nature, too, was having a siesta and would only rouse herself again in the cool of evening. Then, the drooping lily-like flowers of the daturas would open wide to breath out their heavy sweetness. I had always been told never to lie under these trees because their scent might overpower me and send me to sleep for ever. I was never even tempted to try because I knew those scented trumpets had an irresistable attraction for ants, and the thought of their dropping down my neck was a sufficient deterrent; I preferred to lie on the dry crackly leaves which littered the ground round the russet and grey stems of the eucalyptus. The scent of eucalyptus oil on one's handkerchief is somewhat suffocating, but breathed out of doors on a roasting hot day, what could be more delightfully refreshing? Lying there on that sizzling after-noon, sticky and uncomfortable and against the advice of my elders and betters who were no doubt relaxing on their beds, I felt sure that the gains far outweighed all the discomforts.

From where I lay, looking up the sloping lawns I could see the three domes of the *palacio*, a flag on the central one, looming large and oriental – some said, ugly against the bright sky. To me they looked enchanting, entirely beautiful and appropriate in their magical surroundings. Below the mass of the *palacio* lay the terraces, their carved stone balustrades covered with jasmine, bougainvillea and other exotics. Above the balustrade and framing the south door

entrance rose a collonade of white pillars with pointed
Moorish-style arches. So entranced was I with these bewitch-
ing sights and sounds that soon I was trying to express my
feelings in words. I wrote my verses down and eventually
showed the effort to Father. He, with his usual sympathy for
any of my 'artistic' productions said he was much impressed,
especially with the fourth verse. I was glad of that because I
had considered it quite good myself though not absolutely
sure what it meant. It went on and on endlessly and very
boringly but I am including two or three verses here, not
because of their poetic merit but because, in spite of the lack
of it, I think they do convey, if only faintly, some of the
fairyland atmosphere of that wonderful garden.

> A hush so deep and breathless
> That Nature seems asleep;
> Only the soughing windfall
> And the little streams that leap
> And ripple in the shadows
> As beneath the trees they creep.
>
> Great flower faces lift their heads
> From depth of languid shade
> In dazzling glory blushing
> For the fragrance they have made
> All in their sleepy innocence
> By ardent sun betrayed.

I am not attempting to write the full story of Monserrate
here; this needs a much more fluent pen and researchful mind
than I possess. I am writing about Monserrate only in as far as
the place affected me, a young girl. The romance of the
rebuilding of the *palacio* and the creation of the botanical
gardens would read like some fairy tale with my great-grandfather as the wizard waving his wand over the countryside,
giving new life to old impoverished family quintas and
employment to the poverty stricken peasants. The story by
Ida Kingsbury called *Cintra Tapestry* will, I hope, when
published supply all the missing detail of mine. Here I can

only give a few bare bones, leaving the more appetising morsels to her.

Sir Francis first saw the place while on his honeymoon in 1841. His wife, Emily Lucas was the third daughter of a wealthy English merchant living in Lisbon in the English community known as the 'Factory'. Sir Francis was greatly struck with the beauty of the then delapidated estate and made up his mind to buy it and rebuild it. Monserrate then belonged to a Frenchman called de Vimes who sub-let it to, amongst others, Byron, for a short time and to that notorious dilettante William Beckford. Beckford seems to have amused himself in his usual manner by sticking towers and domes on the old building and then, tiring of it presumably, went on to the creation of that fantastic place, Fonthill Abbey in Wiltshire.

Thus it was not until 1856 that Sir Francis was able to buy the estate and very soon after began the rebuilding and recreation of the property under the supervision of Mr. James Knowles, F.R.I.B.A. He filled the Moorish-styled *palacio* with a wonderful collection of pictures and treasures, helped and advised by his old friend Sir Charles Robinson, Surveyor of the Royal Collection. With another old friend, William Stockdale, artist and designer, he made the world-famous Botanical Gardens, bringing trees and shrubs there from all over the world. As witness to his achievements in Portugal and especially for his beneficence to the poor of Lisbon, he was created Visconde de Monserrate by the grateful Portuguese monarch. We were, of course, being constantly reminded of him, not only by the busts in marble and bronze in hall and library but by the initials and dates on tanks and fountains all over the estate. Enormously enlarged photographs of him, too, decorated the parlour of many a humble dwelling.

This then was the exotic play-land devised by my great-grandfather for the pleasure of his family and friends. Of course I never saw him in that setting, nor was I ever there

with my grandfather either. All my life I had been familiar
with stories of Portugal and the parties at Monserrate but it
was not till I was thirteen that the great adventure came my
way. This was mainly because my brother was considered too
young to embark on such a journey before he was four;
therefore my sister and I had to wait.

What an upheaval it was, that first, and in fact all the
ensuing trips. We travelled first class, though there was
nothing ultra luxurious in the cabin accommodation. It was
an immensely exciting experience for me never having even
seen a passenger ship before. The *Aragon* was the first of the
Royal Mail liners which was honoured with our presence;
11,000 tons, I think she was. I can remember mother
wandering in and out of our cabins in her Jaeger dressing-
gown to see how we were standing up or rather lying down to
the very rough seas in the Bay. She fed us on biscuits and
apples and we survived remarkably well. I forget the exact
number in our party but probably near the twenty mark
including nurses and maids. Two of our attendants were
sisters, Kate Thorne who looked after Rachel and Francis and
Alys Thorne who coped with Olga and myself and any other
young thing of our ages. Alys told me the other day when
reminiscing about these trips that she also had the unenviable
job of counting and checking all the innumerable cases with
which we travelled. In addition to a totally unnecessary
amount of clothing, half of which we could have well done
without, there were crates of Malvern water, tins of special
foods and supplies of medicines. Mother could not possibly
allow us to eat foreign foods and drink strange water, though
this was probably far purer, coming as it did straight off the
top of the Sierra, than our tap water at home. So poor Alys's
responsibility was to count all these precious cases on every
possible occasion – probably never less than thirty of them
– and always she was in a state of anxiety lest on arrival one
of them should be found missing.

On the quay at Lisbon we were met by Mr. Oram, the

estate manager. We picked him out at once from the seething crowds, a small dark man clad in a white suit and panama hat. Everything would have been arranged by him from then onwards as for a royal progress, no hitches or tedious delays, nothing to do but enjoy oneself.

Father adored this royal progress and as the little train dragged its slow way up the line to Cintra Station, about twenty miles from Lisbon our excitement mounted with every inch it climbed. 'There's the Pena, look, children', he cried and we craned our necks out of the windows just able by looking almost vertically upwards to catch a glimpse of the fantastic castle perched above us on the skyline of the Serra. 'Lo, Cintra's glorious Eden intervenes' he quoted joyously as the train shuddered to a halt.

To meet us there were carriages and wagonettes; the carriage and best pair for the Visconde and Viscondessa, that is father and mother and driven by the agent's son. The one driven by Carlos, the so-called coachman was designated for us, being family. This was a very exciting climax to our journey, for Carlos, while awaiting our arrival at the station would have passed the time by 'partaking well but most unwisely'. With strange cries and hisses of encouragement to his mules we would leap forward at full gallop clutching hats and belongings as we tore along the dangerously narrow, winding road to Monserrate. I remember on one occasion, I think it must have been on our return one evening from a Lisbon bull-fight, being rather surprised when our dear Alys Thorne arrived at the front entrance very red in the face and looking a bit abashed with her arms twined round Carlos's ample waist; she had found it necessary to anchor him to his driving seat all the way from Cintra station, some three miles away.

On our arrival at the entrance gates there would be a great crowd of tenants gathered. Well to the fore stood the lodge keeper José Percebo, his wife and numerous progeny. As the carriages stopped, José stepped forward followed by the crowd. Father and mother extended their hands in royal fashion. José seized them, covering them with tears of joy and garlicky kisses. Everyone else followed suit, even our hands were grabbed and wept over, rather to our embarrassment.

Father, however, was in his element, rising to the occasion regally. Pleasurable emotion affected him strongly; his nostrils began to flap and his eyes grew moist, and I am sure he was genuinely happy to see their joy. He could speak and certainly understood Portuguese moderately well but now he did not attempt to cope with the torrential flow of words that surged around him but contented himself and everyone else with smiles, nods and hand shakes.

At last José, much to our relief, with a happy grin that revealed his apparently one and only tooth, flung open the gates and the cavalcade dashed through, gaining speed as it swept down the steep, winding drive. Sometimes the drivers remembered to put on the brakes, but if not, as seemed more usually the case in the hot excitement of the moment, the poor animals had to sit on their backsides and slither round the dangerous bends. We rushed past the stables at full gallop waving to the schoolchildren assembled outside under the watchful eye of Mrs. Oram, the agent's wife who was also the schoolmistress. We dashed beneath the terra-cotta Indian archway, swung round the circular fountain and came to rest at the foot of the stone steps leading up to the front door. We had arrived! Julio and Maria, the small rotund, smiling butler and his handsome housekeeper wife and the rest of the staff, not forgetting old Henriques the head gardener and a host of underlings stood waiting. More hand kissings and tears of joy. We lacked only a red carpet and a band to complete the picture of a royal occasion.

The circular stone fountain at the foot of the steps splahed away merrily. The huge old Cork tree on one corner of the terrace stretched its branches over the two stone tables and the Italian well-head; the hammock hung invitingly from one of its boughs. There, next day, we would be able to lie gazing across the miles of intervening greenery to the dark line of the Serra on which Pena castle rose sharply clear-cut against the sky. Big tubs of Strelitzias with orange and blue heads like the crests of African Kavarondo cranes made gay splashes of colour on either side of the steps. In the other corner of the terrace rose the slender Ailanthus, the Tree of Heaven which had been planted by King Edward VII. There had been a second one planted beside it by the doomed King Carlos which had died and soon afterwards he himself had been assassinated.

We walked up the last steps into the cool marble entrance hall to the accompaniment of weird cries from the peacocks no doubt wondering what was going on. We young ones and nurses had rooms in the upper part of the central dome, the lower part being occupied by guests. Our parents slept in the Tower rooms over the entrance. From the octagonal gallery which ran right round the central dome we could look down over the balustrade of white Delhi alabaster upon a fountain of white Carrara marble. This fountain splashed and tinkled day and night spattering crystal drops on the bunches of flowers arranged daily for our delight by Henriques and his black stocking-capped minions in their grey cotton trousers and blouses. Marble statues filled every niche of the long, cool corridor with here and there wavy green palms and other plants to temper their cold white nakedness. Some of the more tender-hearted of the guests (and I remember sharing their opinion when older) did not consider they had adequate protection, so, in the morning, after a jolly party the night before, there could be seen rows of cosily dressed Apollos and Dianas in the latest Parisian outfits. But father did not appear to be greatly amused. The third dome at the end of this seventy or so yards corridor, was entirely filled by the music room in which I spent so many happy hours playing on the fine Bechstein. This was a breathtaking room with marble pillars and moorish arches beneath the domed, elaborately decorated, plaster ceiling covered in gold leaf. A magnificent chandelier hung in the centre, priceless vases stood in the alcoves and beautiful rugs lay on the floor. Sofas, chairs and tables were of a very hard black Indian wood, unusual, but terribly uncomfortable to sit on. But what a room for sound! At that time I was studying Beethoven's sonatas; I still have that book, much marked and looking its age. What joy hearing such music in such surroundings. Unfortunately, from the point of view of concentrated practice there was no door to the room to keep the sounds from rolling down the corridor so that I was never left for long without somebody or other creeping in to listen. Father would often come in to sit on one of the knobbly chairs or on a hard piano stool to play duets with me. There were always some gifted musicians among our friends and many wonderful hours have I enjoyed listening to somebody playing or singing.

Father had inherited many of his grandfather's gifts and characteristics in his concern for the welfare of the peasant and for his knowledge and appreciation of all beautiful things. He was a marvellously kind host to his guests and he and mother were always arranging excursions and outings for their pleasure.

As for the meals which mother organised with the help of Mr. Oram who came up to the *palacio* every morning from his *quinta* in the valley, never since those gargantuan repasts have I seen anything to rival them. These creations were handed to us as we sat round the long dining table by our dear Julio, beaming with pleasure. I can see him now, a short rotund little Portuguese balancing on one hand high over his head a huge dish filled with these delights. Short of breath from such unaccustomed exertions, he would puff and hiss down our necks as he lowered the food under our noses all the while encouraging us with ecstatic praise as to its merits and urging us on to over-eat quite shamelessly. What a delightful, cheery, little man he was, devoted to the family and as proud of the place as if he owned it. Julio knew where everything was, he was quite indispensible, or so he hoped we would realise; and up to a point he was and we did. 'O, Julio', echoed through the place continually and Julio would come running up importantly, grinning happily. Maria was the same. For many years she had been housekeeper there and 'A, Maria' was the incessant cry. Dressed in black with a little lace apron she looked smart but a trifle forbidding with her greying hair and sallow complexion. Through Maria, who of course knew everybody in the neighbourhood, mother engaged various young girls to work in the house, many of them members of Maria's own family.

It was a happy day for us when a young girl of fifteen from the village of Gallemares came to help with us. Her name was Laura Saraiva, one of a large impoverished family living in the valley. When we returned to England we took Laura with us to help in the nursery and teach us Portuguese. She came back with us when we went out to Monserrate again in 1914 but she insisted on returning with us to her beloved England. The First World War then came and for the next five years Laura had to stay put with us. During her enforced exile she learnt to speak perfect English, of course, leaving us well behind in our Portuguese. On our next visit in 1919 at the end of the War, we brought Laura back to her family and in 1920 she was married to her faithful waiting Antonio.

The wedding in Cintra was a gay affair but first of all came the civil marriage in Laura's home in the valley. Mother did not come to Monserrate that year so I, as the eldest of the family was asked to be Laura's godmother which seemed to be one of the necessities for a Portuguese marriage. My father, likewise, was godfather to sustain the bridegroom.

The cavalcade set off from Laura's home for the church in Cintra, myself sitting in the grand family carriage with a very emotional bride who clutched my hand all the way, blushing, smiling and weeping alternately. I sat with my arm round the plump little figure smothered in white lace and getting very worried at her apparent distress till in the midst of sobs and sighs she blurted out ecstatically, 'Oh, Miss Vera, how very happy I am, but I am so sad to think that I may never see dear England again'.

My father was just behind us in another carriage with the blushing bridegroom who was so overcome by the grandeur of the occasion, having the Visconte to hold his hand and lead him to the altar, that he couldn't utter a word but sat with a fixed grin on his round face, his moustachios quivering with emotion.

The Cintra Church was packed with the families of Laura and Antonio and friends from Gallemares and Cintra and soon we were throwing rose petals at each other and the happy pair departed for their honeymoon into the Hotel Centrale in the Square, just round the corner, which for the next fifty years or so they ran together as a successful venture. Antonio died a few years ago, but Laura, still very much the Grande Dame of Cintra, carries on the business with the able help of her son and his wife. While not exactly qualifying as a three star hotel, the place has a character of its own, each bedroom has now a bathroom attached and is kept in spotless condition, the cuisine being overwhelming in quantity if not in quality. Laura's knowledge of English stands her in very good stead as she welcomes boat-loads of tourists from the liners calling in at Lisbon for a day's sight-seeing. She can now speak French as well and has a smattering of German.

It is difficult to recognise in the dignified figure of ample proportions with white hair, our small, dark-haired nursery-maid of so many years ago.

12

Round and About

❮━━━❯

Nearly all our expeditions were taken in carriage, wagonnette or on mule-back, not counting our immediate wanderings on foot around the property. We were for ever setting out for long rambles here, there and everywhere, but it was really a question of time. Having climbed slowly up the drive under the hot sun to the entrance gates on to the main road which led to Cintra in one direction, to Collares in the other, we more often chose to plunge into the bathing lakes on the other side of the road. This occupied the whole morning and very pleasant it was. Here was a hut, a boat and boulders from which to dive into the soft brown water which came pouring from the high Serra above, and with hot, smooth slabs of rock on which to lie roasting in the sun along with the lizards.

To make sure that his friends were enjoying themselves to the full and not wasting a moment of their time, father arranged an excursion to some place of interest almost every day. I suppose the biggest one was a trip to Lisbon to see churches and museums and, above all, a bull-fight. For these outings we were driven to Cintra station in the carriages and mule-carts which met us again in the evening. The exciting drive back along the narrow road with a very merry Carlos driving us was a fitting end to a wonderful day.

Bull-fights have been seen and described by so many people that I will only say how my first one affected me. A brilliant, colourful scene, the bull-ring — a solid mass of excited faces. The seats very hard, the sun relentlessly beating down on us. I remember vividly the beautiful, superbly trained horses ridden by the superbly dressed picadores galloping round the arena closely chased by the tormented bull. The picador's object was to drive his dart into the bull's neck muscles without letting the bull's horns even graze his horse. Should one of these horses be injured, the whole arena erupted in howling displeasure at the incompetence of the picador's performance. A very different version of the savagery of the Spanish bull-fight. There was beauty, too, in watching the *matadores* and the *banderilleros* in their brightly coloured silks and satins skimming over the arena like so many coloured butterflies. All this makes an unforgettable picture. The ethics of a bullfight did not bother me unduly then, but I know I did *not* enjoy watching the bull, looking like a porcupine with the be-ribboned shafts of the darts sticking out around his neck, the blood trickling down onto the sand and hearing his squeals of frustration and pain. It was impossible to avoid seeing him even though I did manage partly to close my eyes when I thought nobody was looking at me. I was immensely relieved when with tinkling bells around their necks a small herd of cows came trotting into the arena to collect their poor exhausted lord and master. Then, after an interval in which the place was cleaned up a bit, fanfares announced the appearance of another bull and the whole thing began all over again. It was an exhausting afternoon for all concerned, onlookers as well as actors, but apart from those who had been hurt or even killed, which did happen sometimes, it had been an exhilarating experience.

Two incidents stand out in my memory, one which might have been serious but which ended in laughter and another which ended in tragedy. As I am sure everybody knows, there is a corridor or passage immediately between the arena barrier and the barrier round the base of the auditorium. It is into this corridor that the hard pressed matadors leap to safety when hotly pursued by the bull; it is also where reporters and photographers can stand in order to get good views of the arena. On this Sunday (bullfights always took place on a Sunday) this particular bull was vastly enjoying himself chasing his too daring tormentors so that they were continually having to run and leap over the barrier, then back again into the arena. The photographer, beneath the black cloak which shaded the lens from the bright sunlight was also enjoying himself snapping the funny scene and everyone was happy and amused. Suddenly the whole auditorium exploded in uproar, yelling and stamping and wildly waving papers and cushions; the bull surprisingly had jumped the barrier and was steadily trotting along the corridor bearing down upon the unsuspecting photographer! Perhaps it was the unusual volume of sound which made the photographer poke his head from under his cloth only to find himself staring straight into the bull's face! With a yell he immediately leapt the barrier into the arena while with savage glee the bull attacked the camera, tossing it in the air to come down a tangled mass all over the place. In its relief the auditorium rocked with laughter and 'olays'. I think after that bull's athletic display he was treated with respect and was very soon collected by his herd of wives and escorted out. A somewhat expensive Sunday afternoon for the photographer!

The other incident I remember so clearly was this. It is the custom in the Portuguese bullfights to bring into the arena a small party of poorly dressed and unarmed men at the end of a fight and their unenviable job is to surround the bull holding him by horns, tail and ears to prove how exhausted the poor animal has become from the treatment he has received from his tormentors. The leader of this suicidal squad has the worst job of the lot. He has to stand alone, hands behind his back waiting till the bull sees him and charges, then to throw himself onto the lowered head between the horns (which incidentally, in Portuguese fights are cork tipped). He is then allowed to twine his arms round them hanging on for dear life till the rest of the gang rush up to hold the bull still. If this manoeuvre is successful they get an ovation and more often than not it is. But sometimes the bull is not as exhausted as he should be and shakes off the clutching men as easily as a swarm of flies. This is what happened on one Sunday when I was there and the poor chap clinging desperately to the horns was powerless to prevent himself from being repeatedly bashed upon the ground. He was killed before the bull could be overpowered. I believe this occupation is considered to be only fit for the down and outs of Lisbon and is very poorly paid. But it must take a brave or a very desperate man indeed to try his luck this way.

When I was considerably older I remember seeing a fine white stallion in the ring and being told it was his last appearance. He had once been gored (by mistake) in the leg and was considered to be too nervous to continue to put up a good show, and I don't wonder. Through strings, pulled effectively by Mr. Oram, we managed to buy this horse and after a while he duly arrived in England. His name was Favorito; he was gentle as a lamb with a ride like an arm chair. We used to ride him along the beach at Studland where he amused onlookers by doing some of his *haute école* stunts. If he happened to appear on the beach at the same time as the local riding school, then goodbye, riding school; a stallion was *not* the thing for an English beach. Poor old Favorito; he had a long peaceful life, far from the clamour of the bull-ring, but in his old age developed a growth in the groin where he had been wounded and had to be destroyed.

There were numerous other expeditions nearer Monserrate nearly all involving some form of transport. The nicest of all, I thought, was the two-mile walk or ride to the Cork Convent over the wild country of the Serra. This strange, beautiful place was a penance monastery which had been built for the Capuchin monks by the de Castro family who owned Penha Verde, a *quinta* near Monserrate. It was occupied by these monks for nearly one hundred years till 1640. It is built into the rock, and the cells are lined with cork. It stands about a thousand feet up on the Serra, completely isolated and camouflaged by outcrops of huge granite boulders. It belonged to the estate and we often visited it though it was rough going for both mules and walkers. But it was immensely worth the effort. The whole area exhaled the hot, earthy smell of pine and cistus, lizards sprawled over the boulders in brilliant blues and greens and carpets of small wild flowers and the tall pale asphodel covered the ground. The track was difficult to find, as most certainly was our goal, the Convento dos Capuchos. No one could have seen it from a distance, nor even guessed where it lay hidden, until they had practically stumbled upon the little entrance between two enormous granite boulders, on one of which was a rough stone cross and a little bell. Probably the mule cart with the picnic and some of the more delicate or lazier of the guests would have arrived first in spite of having had to make a long detour by a rough road; the riding party was by far the better off, arriving hot, but not exhausted, while the stalwart walkers panted along (it was uphill all the way) both hot and exhausted but proud of their endurance.

We ate our picnic to the cool accompaniment of water dropping into stone basins, seated round stone tables in the open air Refectory. The walls there are covered with ferns and mosses, while overhead the gnarled limbs of many a lichen-covered Cork tree meet and entwine in a Rackham-like embrace. Haunted? Oh, without a doubt. I would not have been surprised to have found the mummified body of an old monk in any of the little cork-lined cells. Where were they buried, anyhow, when they died? 'Deep in yon cave did old Honorious dwell', wrote Bryon in *Childe Harolds' Pilgrimage* and this we quoted as we climbed down the steep path, clambering over the big boulders to peer into his deep, dark living tomb. I couldn't believe he had sat there till he died 'in the hope of reaching Heaven by making Earth a Hell', some thirty or more years. Perhaps he had crept out when the other monks were asleep to wander about the peaceful alleys in the moonlight. He certainly seemed very much alive the night I remember so clearly when we decided to walk up there.

It was a sudden decision we had taken after dinner, one breathlessly hot night. The moon was brilliant, as were the stars, glittering like sequins on a dark blue veil. There was a fitful breeze blowing, bringing to our eager nostrils the hot, intoxicating scent of pine and cistus. The white shapes of granite boulders sprawling over the hillside looked like sleeping monsters in the moonlight. Both Father and Mother walked with us that night but I forget who else. Father had taken off his jacket and loped along in shirt, trousers and braces, the Wand of Office in his hand. This 'wand' was a long walking stick with a silver head used by the Viscondes. One by one we straggled into the refectory, hot but happy. We drank gratefully from our cupped hands of the ice-cold water which tumbled into the stone basins. I was much moved by the serenity of the quiet place, the soft moon-light accentuating every dark corner. The melodious splashing of water falling into the fountain in the old Monks' garden seemed like a requiem for their souls' repose.

The Cork Convent by Moonlight

Peace, and a cloudless vault of blue
With soft winds sweeping;
Night, with her flashing stars
And moonbeams creeping.

Great white, shadowy shapes
Couchant on hillside bare
And gentle water dripping,
Making music there.

Dim shades of living things unseen,
Of mem'ries long since gone
Haunt the breathless avenues
Or sighing, move alone.

This lovely spot no longer belongs to the family; with the *palacio* it is now owned by the State and I cannot help wondering how much longer it will retain its simple, haunting beauty which touches all hearts. Now that the whole Serra has been thickly planted by the Forestry Department with big motor-roads across it, the remote secrecy of the hidden monastery has to some extent disappeared and hordes of sightseers arrive from all over the country in char-a-bancs.

We sometimes made excursions by tram along the valley down to the sea. We walked down the drive on the north-west side of the *palacio* through groves of oranges and lemons until we came to the boundary chain stretching across the drive in charge of the blind guard. Hearing our voices he would snatch off his stocking cap, fumbling for our hands to kiss. Then bowing low he would unhook the chain for us to pass. I was, I think, needlessly sorry for him because in other circumstances he would never have had a job at all. Having reached the main road we all sat in a gully in the hot sun and dust awaiting the arrival of the little tram. With clanging bell and much clattering and squeaking it sooner or later appeared, swinging from side to side and we climbed in amid a crowd of garlic-chewing natives.

Preia dos Mesanges (Bay of Apples) in those days was a quiet little bay with fine sands and huge Atlantic rollers. The under-tow was much too fierce for any real swimming but we were allowed to wallow in the surf. Now, alas, the Bay has a swimming pool, a tea place and the usual crowds.

Sometimes we drove or rode to Collares (where most of the wine is made) in the opposite direction to Cintra and there we watched the grapes being trodden. There were rows and rows of gigantic barrels, a heady smell of wine and sweat and the top halves of men's bodies bobbing up and down in the barrels as they trod the pulp. Perspiration poured off them into the juice (that's what gives it its 'bouquet' said the know-alls) and their breathing was stertorous. I was told that when at last they were lifted out they immediately fell down flat, tight as ticks.

Going into Cintra itself could be fun especially if one rode

in on mule-back by the track below the *palacio*, thus avoiding
the road. We would sometimes do this very early in the
morning when the cook went in by mule-cart to market. And
in the square where Laura and Antonio's hotel stands there is
the beautiful old royal palace with its two enormous
chimneys like the Kentish oast chimneys and the fine rooms
and floors covered with lovely coloured tiles, *azulejos* as they
were called. How anybody could have wanted to live in
another palace as the royal family apparently did when they
built the preposterous magician's castle — the Pena — I fail to
understand. True its position is fabulous, perched high on the
sky-line of the towering Serra and the views from there are
breathtaking. But the Palace itself is quite awful unless one
admires a mixture of German, Victorian, Manualine and
Scottish architecture and the furnishings are equally unattractive. All the same the climb up there was always stimulating
and especially the descent down the steep winding roads with
ultra hair-pin bends. As usual the carriages were driven down
at breakneck speed, the animals helping to brake by sitting
on their haunches and skidding round the bends.

How pleasant then, after such exertions was the plunge
into the soft water of the bathing lake on our return. Then
crossing the road to the entrance gates amid bows and smiles
from José we would wend our way down to the *palacio* by
devious routes pausing to gather up some of the scarlet
berries covering the ground around the arbutus trees, some of
which we ate though rather unenthusiastically, being tasteless
and boring. But we never tired of gathering the eucalyptus
berries of all shapes in hues of green to grey to brown to
make up into necklaces. I have some still and I have only to
plunge them into very hot water to bring out their delicious
scent which takes me back again to that paradise of gardens.

Changing for dinner that night everybody would find on
his or her dressing-table the most enchanting button-hole, no
two alike, the work of Julio and Maria. This was a nightly
ritual. It was quite a minor excitement to see what each

night's thought would produce and compare merits over dinner.

Memories of Monserrate are legion, sounds and scents perhaps the strongest and inseparable from any thoughts of the place. What could be more exciting and beautiful than dawn as seen from Monserrate ledge? This ledge as we called it was accessible from most of the bedroom windows, in fact it ran the full length of the building round the domes. It was quite broad, wide enough for anyone to sleep thereon if they wished. This is what we often did though I don't think it was a very popular escapade with the adults. We dragged our mattresses off our beds and climbed with them out of the windows. As a precaution we tied ourselves by our dressing gown cords onto the small stone pillars which surrounded the window frames. It was lucky there were no sleep-walkers among us with a sheer drop of some fifty feet to the ground. We lay there listening to the fading sounds in the valley as the sky darkened, the soft scented wind just moving the tops of the great cedars which seemed very little higher than we were.

I found it impossible to sleep soundly and was always wide awake in time to see dawn breaking behind the dark, sharp outline of the Serra. Almost before I could sit up to stare and marvel at this miracle, the red sun showed over the dark mass of the land and with incredible speed mounted into the sky. Then the dogs began to bark, the cocks began to crow and far away I could hear the groans of the ox-cart wheels as they creaked their slow arthritic way in the valley below. Before very long a new sound would break on the still morning — the postman's horn, now far, now near as he wound his way up the zig-zag road to the *palacio*.

Dawn from Monserrate Lodge

> The cry of a bird, a crag all lone,
> The sigh and rustle in the waking trees
> And the purple folds of Night are gone
> To shroud some land beyond the seas.

Voices of Nature, murm'ring faint
Grow sharper, stronger as the wind sweeps by,
Till Phoebus mounts his rushing steeds
And drives all furious 'cross the sky.

Sight is indeed precious but a blind person would have no need to lament his lack of vision if his nose and ears were keen. Blindfold me and drop me onto the end of the terrace on a hot summer evening when the sun is going down into the Atlantic in a blaze of crimson; I will tell you where I am when I hear the faint barking of dogs, the creak of ox-wagon wheels in the darkening valley and smell the warm air heavy with eucalyptus. Blindfold me again, stop up my ears as well and leave me on the rough sides of Monte Bedel, our little mountain on the Serra; who could fail to detect on the fitful winds the salt tang of the Atlantic mingling with the sweet smell of warm gum cistus and the sun-drenched pine?

13

Studland

⬤━━━━⬤

We went to the sea-side every summer. A change of air was considered a good thing, especially the ozone we inhaled from the sea air and sea weed. Very diligently, mother went searching for pleasant beaches and good accommodation for us. This was not such an undertaking then as it is today for the roads were comparatively free from traffic; there were far fewer bodies about which made travelling easier. And at least there was always room and to spare on our lovely beaches and accommodation did not have to be booked months ahead. In this respect we were luckier than some because our parents always rented a whole house, which I suppose was reasonable with our sized family. And as we took the cook and a maid in addition to the nursery staff, what could be simpler?

The modern child, blasé and bored as country after country flashes by beneath its nose as the jets roar across the world, could never understand what excitement we enjoyed when our trunks were brought out to be packed for our little train journey; for us it was a truly great adventure.

A whole first class carriage was reserved for us, but before we could entrain an important 'ceremony' took place. The footman was sent ahead to disinfect it. Behold, therefore, William or Alfred or whomsoever, having first carefully shut all the windows, directing with determination and thoroughness his spray of formalin all over the upholstery and especially into the many dirty little corners in which a germ might be lying in wait for us. His task accomplished, I suppose he aired the carriage before we arrived. I wonder what the station-master and porters thought of such goings on?

Mother usually went on ahead with cook or housemaid to get the house and beds properly aired. Nannie followed with us and nursery maid or governess or both, the following day. Mother insisted on such a regular routine that nothing, not even a train journey, was allowed to break it. We ate our lunch in the carriage but in a less convential way than usual. Cold chicken we held in our fingers (previously sponged and dried by our nurserymaid), cold rice pudding dug out of the enamel dish with our spoons with cold apple purée from a glass jar with a screwed-on top. After that, we were stretched out on the seats on rugs for our usual rest.

One event of which I did not approve was when nannie opened the round tin footbath which had a lid and was firmly strapped down and which was filled to the brim with Francis's nappies and the potty and probably other things as well. Nannie pulled the blinds down while Francis sat on his pot, after which performance she opened the window and emptied it onto the track. I could never understand how nannie could possibly have known if the next-door carriage windows were closed. And I was always in a dither lest the guard or the ticket collector might come in. I remember very little about the places we visited. I know we went to Robin Hood's Bay, Gorleston, Hopton, Colwyn Bay and Westgate and maybe others which I have forgotten. Then, when I was nine, mother discovered Studland in the Isle of Purbeck, and that was the end of our flittings. For the first two summers we rented the rectory (1908 and 1909). Then father bought Hill Close which, at that time, belonged to the playwright and artist, Sutro, and had been designed for him by the architect Voysey in 1896. In this house on the hill with its grey Purbeck stone roof and tall chimneys, we spent every ensuing holiday except when we went to Monserrate and it became our much-loved second home.

And so we travelled from Waterloo to Swanage every summer in our formalin sprayed carriage and on the recently devised single line from Wareham. Excitement grew as the little train crawled into Swanage station. For me, it reached fever pitch when, having climbed down onto the platform clutching (of course) our spades and buckets and passed through the ticket office, I beheld my much admired Mr. Loveless from Studland standing by his wagonette. Tired, but happy, we climbed in sitting opposite each other; nurses, luggage and dog piled in, too, and we were off. If I had been allowed to sit by Loveless on the box my happiness was complete. Loveless had fair hair and a lovely fair moustache and I adored him. He was a kind, gentle man, especially nice to children. I used to linger on the roads around the village when out walking in the hope of meeting him. With spirits soaring, we wound our way along the white dusty road to Studland. When we came to the hill going past the golf course (a car would hardly notice it) we were told to get out and walk to help the horse. This did not surprise us, in fact we thought it fun trudging behind the cart. So while Loveless remained on the box, we all pushed at the back. Arriving at the top with the horse puffing heavily, we climbed in and started on the last mile down hill to Studland, in those days to all intents and purposes the end of the road from Swanage. Beyond the last house (Knoll House) a rough sandy track wound its way across the heath to the harbour where if you wanted to go to Sandbanks, Poole or Bournemouth you were rowed across in Davis's little dinghy.

Few visitors came to Studland when I first knew it except the yearly faithfuls; there was only one little hotel, the Bankes' Arms, no day trippers cluttering up the sandy beaches and, of course, no cars or car parks. The old Norman church was, quite rightly, the centre of village interest; there was a farm with a tithe barn, the base of the village cross and quite a few old thatched cottages. The Manor had been built by the Lord of the Manor, Mr. Bankes, to accommodate his

large growing family. Previously they had lived at Knoll
House.

For the first two days after our arrival we were not
allowed to bathe even if there happened to be a heat wave;
we had to allow time for our systems to get adjusted to the
change of air, for sea air was inclined to upset the liver, or so
authority decreed. Therefore we waited, fuming and grumb-
ling until the third day arrived, when, if the weather was
considered suitable we were allowed to go into the sea for a
very quick dip. The rule was that the back of the head and
neck must be wetted directly we stepped into the water and
never a second bathe, one was considered enough. A quick
run up and down the beach afterwards clad in a warm jersey
and munching a biscuit completed the proceedings. Oh, yes,
we were very well looked after – perhaps too much so. Our
lives were ordered and arranged so that we never had to think
for ourselves, only obey orders. Mother had very decided
views on our upbringing as most good mothers have and was
never forgetful of what she considered her duty towards her
children's well-being.

How lovely that beach was then with so few other people
besides ourselves to enjoy it. Sometimes I look down from
the garden of our friends, the Andersons, on the cliffs onto
the sandy bay below, trees and grass almost to the water's
edge at high tide with the curve of the white cliffs running
out to the Old Harry Rocks and try to re-live the scenes of
our childhood.

We had a small hut on the bank but no boat till we were
much older. Sometimes we hired a row boat from Mr. Payne
who kept a few for that purpose. As I remember him them,
Mr. Payne was an old man with lovely silky white hair. He
was always dressed in navy blue trousers and jersey and
smoked a pipe. Until a few years ago his nephews, Albert and
Gus Payne, now both dead, carried on the business. Mother
was terribly anxious while we were out in the boat. Looking
back from our bobbing craft never more than a hundred

yards off shore, we could see her striding up and down the beach casting anxious glances at us and nervously puffing at her cigarette in its long ivory holder. She looked like Robinson Crusoe must have looked, a real castaway, in a pair of long navy blue bloomers down to the calf, a jersey or shirt and a large shady felt hat. Her red hair rippled down to her shoulders. She had to wear elastic stockings because of her varicose veins and when she went in to swim she wore a serge outfit edged with white braid as we did. Those bathing dresses were hateful, I well remember, because the water took simply ages to permeate the stuff and made the first dip more unpleasant than it need have been because we never got wet in a flash, only in trickles. When we first ventured into the sea we were tied at intervals on to a rope so that mother or nannie could keep a grip on our floundering forms and haul us out quickly if we went under or swallowed too much. Yes, bathing was an event and taken very seriously. I suppose it was still rather a novelty and was regarded more as a health-giving occupation than as something to enjoy for its own sake. As we grew older, we learnt to swim but none of us were ever much good except Rachel who enjoyed diving off the boat and the raft which form of amusement I disliked intensely. In the green twilight of the underworld of the sea I was hopelessly lost. In a panic I would kick out wildly wondering whether I was going the right way and when at last my head broke surface I could have sworn I had been under for hours and all but drowned.

Father would usually come down for the weekends to join us on the beach. In a serge navy blue bathing suit which reached halfway down his pale stick-like legs, he would venture in for a swim. He swam much better than any of us but without embellishments and all we could see of father once he got going was his shiny bald head like a mooring buoy bobbing over the waves far out in the Bay.

But look, who are these two sinister looking figures shuffling along the beach from below the cliffs? I had been watching them for some time and a chill (not from my recent bathe) crept down my spine. Throwing dignity to the winds we cluster round the grown-ups hardly daring to raise our eyes as these unsavoury looking creatures draw near. Both are in rags and tatters; the one with a large felt hat low over his eyes has a big, white face turned heavenwards as he squints down his nose at the sand beneath his feet which he taps as he walks with a long stick held in one hand: with the other hand he clutches the arm of the other scarecrow who has a bilious yellow face and a bulging sack over his shoulder. These two 'buddies' shuffle past us and thankful I am to see the backs of them. I was always in fear of meeting them on our walks through the village, though quite unnecessarily I think, because apart from their terrifying appearance I can't remember hearing anything really bad about them. The squinting one with the flat white face was called 'Old Moley' because he was nearly blind and his yellow-faced friend was Hopkins. They both lived in the village and I have been told that when Old Moley became too unsanitary he was forced into a bath and scrubbed, by whom I can't say. He always looked filthy to me but perhaps I only saw him just before bath night. Hopkins was more able to look after himself, in fact, I think he must have poached for both because I never saw either of them without a bulging sack, very suggestive of corpses.

Mother was very much a child in her love of dressing up and pretending. At one time we all had Red Indian suits, a wig-wam and the rest. We played Hiawatha games all over the garden and on the cliffs where her friends Peter Alexander and the Smalls had their caravans. 'Smalley' was an artist and later painted the portrait of me now hanging in our home. We would sit round the camp fires singing while mother played her concertina. Rachel acted her part as a 'brave' most realistically taking prisoners, scalping them and smoking peacepipes. My role always seemed to be that of the dirty old squaw left behind to keep the homefires going in the wigwam. Scouts were all the rage at one time when with proper scout hats, whistles, poles and badges we 'tracked' across the heath. But the highlight of every August holiday was (and still is) the Flower Show. During the first two Augusts when we were renting the rectory, the Flower Show was held in the field opposite, across the road. In the spring this field was a glory to behold, sheets of yellow and purple crocus covering it like a mosaic. Tragically, this glory vanished during the War when the field was ploughed up. On the Flower Show day that field was packed with tents, flags and streamers everywhere and the thrilling throb and bellow from the enthusiastic Corfe Castle band rang through our heads all the afternoon. During one of those rectory holidays our parents had a most unusual holiday themselves; they went to Russia, leaving Bow-wow in charge of us. Every so often postcards arrived from that romantic land, usually of troicas sparkling with frost and of peasants in glittering national dress.

It was during their absence that for the first and only time I plucked up courage to write to my mother to implore her support against what I considered to be nearly unbearably unjust treatment. For some small misdemeanour (I failed to pass the cake to my neighbour before helping myself) I was deprived of my slice and sent to bed. I felt the punishment exceeded the crime and very greatly daring and full of righteous wrath wrote to my mother blurting out all my pent-up feelings of long-suffered tyranny. 'We are living in a community,' wrote Mother in her reply, 'and each of us must remember our duty to our neighbour.' Poor mother, what other line could she take? To question Bow-wow's authority could only encourage rebellion, however much justified. I was disappointed but not really surprised. If only she could have known what we endured. Poor Olga suffered more than I did; being older than me and an outsider her punishments were that more severe. I remember that awful day – Flower Show day it was – what crime had she committed that merited banishment to bed for the whole afternoon? There, imprisoned in her room with the Dragon on guard near by, she had to stay, listening to the tantalising 'boomphs' from the field opposite and not all her heartbroken tears, nor my pleadings, melted that heart of stone.

Before father installed the small electric light engine we, of course, had only oil lamps. The strongest memory I have of winter evenings at Hill Close is the smell of oil. In addition to the reading lamps which were brought into the studio which was used by the whole family as a living room, there were small oil lamps hanging on landings and staircase walls. When we went up to bed we were allowed to carry one of these with us and light our candles when we got to our rooms. Smelly lamps and guttering candles were not conducive to loitering while undressing; shadows on walls and in dark corners were not comforting. But in the summer holidays it was quite the opposite. We went to bed with the temperature mounting steadily as we climbed the stairs. Due to the steep angle of the sloping roofs and the heavy Purbeck stone tiles each room became oven-like after a hot, sunny day. When I could not sleep I would stand by the open window or perch on the windowsill inhaling the sweet night smells, enchanted by the vigorous chirring of the crickets and watching the changing light on the waters of the Bay. On cloudless nights I could see the dark outline of Ballard Down running along the skyline and dropping down to the Old Harry rocks with here and there spots of light between the trees coming from windows in the village of other late bedders like myself. Paths of pale moonlight lay across the darkened sea.

Hill Close is built on higher ground than the rest of the Village so that, in those early days before the trees grew enormous towering over and around the little house we could feast our eyes unimpeded upon a full half circle of beauty, north, east and southwards.

The garden was smallish and kept simple with mostly lawns and rough grass and no smart flower beds. At the lower end there were vegetables, soft fruits and apple trees. There was a sprawling rockery at the north end of the studio seemingly tumbling onto the moors below. When it was fine enough we had our breakfast outside on a splendid circular brick lay-out sheltered by growing trees and bathed in the rising sun. But before this a little ceremony took place beside the full-size white-painted flag-staff standing near the house. Mother would appear with her concertina to lead the way like the Pied Piper with everybody trooping after her till we arrived at the grassy knoll and gathered expectantly beside the pole. Punctually at eight o'clock (how did mother hit off the right moment?) she extended her concertina in a long drawn-out chord at which all present stood smartly to attention, hands raised at the salute. The youngest person there (more often than not, Francis, much to our chagrin) slowly pulled the Union Jack up to the top of the pole while everyone else burst into the National Anthem. This was a daily ceremony, wet or fine. The Jack was pulled down with less ceremony at sun-set by anybody who remembered. Later, when we had outgrown the al fresco breakfasts, father filled that space with a fine old Venetian well-head of which he was very fond. It is now in our garden near Corfe Castle.

When we first went to live at Hill Close there was no tennis court, so father decided to level part of the sloping lawns into what we liked to call a cricket pitch. This was where we laid about us with a bat and ball – in fact in due time this pitch could boast a proper 'net' in which the victim stood to be bowled at. Much later, when I was a boarder at Sherborne School for Girls and had managed to get myself into the School XI as wicket keeper, I could think of little else but batting and bowling and being bowled to in the net. This was pleasantly unexacting as played among ourselves because we all seemed to h e the same standard of inefficiency. But it was a very different kettle of fish when the captain of the Winchester XI came to stay.

Humphrey Bingham was the son of a family friend,

General Sir Francis Bingham, a very distinguished soldier who became head of the Commission of Control in Berlin at the end of the Great War. Humphrey very often spent part of his school holiday with us at Studland and, naturally, we were thrilled and proud when this successful young man condescended to play cricket with us, mostly all females and certainly younger than he. But Humphrey was as nice as he looked and 'tempered the wind to the shorn lamb', though now and then his enthusiasm and prowess for the game got the upper hand and he forgot he was bowling to a poor quaking female in the net. Many bumps and bruises were our portion but not for anything would we have forgone them.

From the start of the war we gave sanctuary, as many others like outselves were able to do, to some of those unfortunates who had fled from war-stricken Belgium. Among the rather mixed bag that was our portion, one family from Brussells became very good friends of ours, the Velluts. Their twins, Jean and Lucette were the same age as Rachel. Jean was killed in the 1939 war but Lucette and her family we still see from time to time. As far as we were concerned the war affected us very little. Except for our refugees and a certain amount of military activity in the village when troops of artillery with their gun-carriages drawn by protesting mules cluttered up the lanes, we lived our sheltered lives much as usual. We were still very young and almost totally absorbed in school life of one sort or another. But there were two at least very shattering shocks, for me, at any rate. One was the long drawn-out anxiety over uncle Maurice who was reported missing in the Gallipoli landings and whose death in June 1915 was subsequently assumed. Mother, knowing how fond I was of him, had very kindly kept me supplied with copies of letters received by grannie from his C.O., the padré and brother officers, describing the shambles of that landing and uncle Maurice's persistent disregard of personal safety in the storming of a Turkish redoubt which was eventually blown up. He was never seen again.

This cloud which accompanied me throughout the earlier part of my school life certainly lay heavily upon me and I suppose helped to drag me out of the egoistical complacency in which I had been reclining, more or less comfortably since early childhood. But it was ultimately the second shock, at the end of the war, that pulled me completely out of my Paradise Garden of immaturity into the brassy world of post-war hysteria masquerading as maturity.

14
Julian

◆━━◆

'Oh to be in Portugal, now that April's here'. Well, so I was and the year was 1914. Later, that same month I was also to be in England in a very different environment and with the shadows fast gathering over Europe's and my carefree days of dalliance.

When I first began writing these sketches I had no intention of including in them such a spine-chilling subject as a boarding school till one day a good friend queried the proposed ending to the book by saying, 'Oh, you can't stop there, people will want to know what happened to you'. I said I couldn't believe that anybody would pass even one sleepless night were they never to hear of me again. However, since I think she really wanted me to write something about my school life, if only because the school I went to is now a famous and successful one and very different from the 'Select Seminary for Young Ladies' in which I languished for four years, I suppose it might be quite amusing reading. Not that I myself can claim any credit for lifting Sherborne School for Girls onto its road to success as that great head-mistress, Miss Mulliner, surely could have done; no, indeed, I might well have been one of the mill-stones round its neck, slowing its progress and certainly only one of the many experimental guinea-pigs with whom she undoubtedly laid the foundations for its present good name.

In comparison with the boarding schools of today, ours could easily be called a prison, or anyhow a very strict enclosed order with rules governing every aspect of life, invisible chains shackling our bid for freedom of action for which our developing personalities naturally craved. In addition to the accepted school routine of 'being summoned by bells' here, there and everywhere and the multitudinous 'must-nots', such as no talking in the passages, no running ditto, lights out, lights on, no poking the nose even half an inch outside the school gates, no this, no that, a novel and incomprehensible threat to our survival hung over our heads in the shape of the inmates of the centuries-old boys' school down in the town. In contrast to our feminine modernity perched on the hill, this old school clustered round its venerable abbey like fledglings round their beautiful mother.

Humbly and gratefully for the honour accorded us, we girls from our Peabody buildings on the hill marched each Sunday down through the town to take our places with downcast eyes in the side aisles of the lovely abbey. All possible encounters with the dangerous inmates of this highly superior boys' school had to be avoided; so as we proceeded sedately 'en croc' along the streets, should one of these creatures be sighted on collision course it was only our duty to cross at once to the other side of the road or, right about turn should both sides be infested with the species.

Some of the girls were lucky enough to have brothers in this hive of masculinity and on Sunday afternoons these curiosities were allowed to call for an incarcerated sister in the Peabody buildings to take her out for a walk. Standing at a window, I watched with interest their timid but courageous approach. They would stand peering anxiously through the bars of the drive gates, for, of course, they were not allowed to walk to the front door nor even to the back, until sooner or later the sister appeared to put them out of their agony.

It was indeed a strange world into which I had been tossed, in startling contrast to the fairyland of Monserrate in which I had so recently spent the two happiest weeks of my life.

I was used to females, of course, but not in such overwhelming quantities. A mass of anything, human or inanimate can be frightening and unattractive, especially if hitherto unfamiliar. The only link with home was Olga who had already been a student at the Domestic house attached to the school for the past two or three terms when I arrived. But we rarely saw much of each other, apart from occasional meetings as we sped about our business (the Domestic Science students were allowed to attend sixth-form classes in different subjects) and of course for the Sunday afternoon walks. I was placed in a House called Dun Holme in the capable, though somewhat intimidating hands, of Miss Moore. There being no dormitory place for me and one or two other newcomers, we were relegated to the overflow house called Greenhill, down in the town. This meant walking back and forth to Dun Holme, about threequarters of a mile each way at least twice daily.

I had hardly managed to adjust myself to this novel existence before I found myself in the midst of a crisis which opened my eyes very wide upon an aspect of life which I had never imagined could assume such immense proportions: one of us was expelled.

All kinds of rumours were flying around as to why this very pretty young thing of fifteen or sixteen, I forget her exact age, could have been so evil as to have been pronounced unfit to associate with us other not quite so pretty young things. One by one we were interviewed by the house mistress and bombarded with questions about our private lives; to whom we wrote besides our parents and from whom we received letters and had we realised the enormity of our attractive school-fellow's crime? I don't think many of us had; I certainly had no idea what exactly she had done and to tell you the truth I never found out for certain. I was a brand new girl and would never have had the temerity to ask; I already knew my place. But from thenceforth we were never allowed to forget that writing to a male creature other than a father or a brother was an offence that might exact the utmost penalty.

Many of us almost certainly had a boy friend or cousin with whom we had been accustomed to share our childhood pleasures and pains and news of mutual interest; now we were forced to admit that writing to such creatures was a wicked thing to do while not really believing it was so. To most of us it all seemed a tremendous fuss about nothing but nevertheless it upset me personally very much, for what would happen now about Julian to whom I had promised to write about my first term's experiences?

Julian had been spending the Easter holidays with us at Monserrate and for me those two or three weeks had held a special magic. We had known Julian's family for years; his father, George Gribble, was a cousin of father's and a valued member of the City firm. There were five children, Julian being the youngest, almost exactly two years older than I was. His nannie, Louisa Simmonds had been passed on to us when Julian had outgrown her and we, the Cooks, had a still growing family in the nursery. Julian and his mother sometimes came to stay with us at Copseham and I can remember feeling very disapproving and rather concerned about Julian (I must then have been about three) because he still wore girlish overalls and coats with his hair in long ringlets. We never got to know each other properly till that spring in Portugal. Julian was then seventeen and at Eton. In my opinion he was a gorgeous person, already six feet three, of splendid physique, with brilliant dark blue eyes. To my amazement this god-like creature seemed to enjoy my company as much as I did his. Together, we wandered through the gardens, swam in the lakes and rode our mules miles over the Serra. Oh yes, Julian was fun and everybody in the party liked him. Alys and Kate Thorne, our maid and nurse were enchanted with him because he did not consider it infra dig to play with our six-year-old brother, Francis; in fact, he seemed to enjoy joining in the pranks. Once Alys remembers they turned on all the wheel taps in the loos. Another time they waited their chance till a smart party was walking innocently around the balcony which ran around the central dome and suddenly switched up the fountain below, usually just trickling politely into its alabaster basin so that everybody got a thorough and unexpected soaking. I watched Julian playing tennis with the grown-ups, whole-hearted in my admiration of his skill. For my age I was a completely unsophisticated creature, even for those times. I had always been treated as a child so I behaved childishly. I couldn't even play tennis, at least not up to Julian's standard. But I played Beethoven's Sonatas to him in that wonderful music room. He loved music and could never have enough. We discussed the books and poems we had read. Julian seemed to have read most of Dickens and adored Kipling. He promised to give me a copy of *The Day's Work* by Kipling because he wanted me to read a story in it called 'The Brushwood Boy'. I wondered then why he liked it so much.

We talked a lot about schools and I confessed all my fears and apprehensions of my coming fate. He tried to reassure me that it wouldn't be that awful, 'really quite good fun at times', he had said (he could well talk, thought I, being one of the shining lights at Eton and already in 'Pop'). He promised to write if I would. I can remember asking him whether he was allowed to stay up for dinner in the holidays with his parents because I wasn't; I had to have my supper in the school-room and then go to bed.

'Don't be such a silly baby', said Julian kindly. 'If you aren't allowed to stay up to dinner in the evening, then I won't either; I'll have mine upstairs like you'. I considered this a very noble thing for anyone to do for someone else and became more adoring than ever.

We leant together over the balustrade at the end of the terrace to watch the red sun sink into the violet rim of the world where the sky fused with the darkening waters of the Atlantic. 'Going, going, gone', we chanted as the red ball dropped swiftly into the sea. It fell as if lowered by an unseen hand on an invisible thread. We promised to remember this last evening whenever we saw a red setting sun. Thus we talked, happy to be young with all life ahead. Or had we?

The next day, Olga and I and Alys with Wag to shepherd us, set off for England. As usual, it was hard to leave that enchanted place; for me, a bigger wrench than ever because Julian was remaining on another week, to help mother bring home the rest of the party. In any case, the new Half at Eton didn't begin for another ten days.

In a few days I was quickly transformed into a new species of animal in a coat and skirt and hard straw boater and deposited in the alien setting in which I was to 'develop' for the next four years. Already Monserrate and Julian and all nice things seemed like a dream.

As soon as I could I put pen to paper and wrote to Julian who was by then back at Eton. The Expelling excitement had yet to come so we had been able to exchange several letters before the decree went forth that we were forbidden to write to any male creature other than a father or a brother. In spite of this, I did manage to get one or two letters to him enclosed in ones to the family, but as it was considered equally wicked and therefore forbidden to receive any back, what was the point? We decided to wait till the holidays.

But those carefree holidays never came, because on 4th August before we could make any plans to meet again, the dark clouds which had long been hanging over our heads, burst and all Europe lay defenceless to a deluge the like of which had never been endured, at least in living memory.

15

School and War

❖

It is said that in one's journey through life many of the
unpleasant things that happen to one tend to be forgotten
and only the nicer events are remembered. This is simply
because the sub-conscious mind rejects, as far as it can,
anything it does not want to remember. In many instances
this is true enough, though when looking back on school life
I cannot actually pin-point any really disastrous or distressing
event, at any rate not of sufficient magnitude to leave a
mark. All the same my overall impression seems to be a grey
one with rather a nasty taste in the mouth. Why this should
be, I can't explain, except that maybe I was a bad mixer. For
one thing I could not bring myself to join in any of the many
entanglements that snarled up throughout the House when,
with heads together in corners, the girls huddled, whispering
and giggling about someone, or something. And for another I
was sure that everybody was laughing at the boots I had to
wear indoors; and my stammer made reading aloud in class a
nightmare in anticipation and in fact. Not that I did not have
some very good friends and some small personal triumphs;
the trouble lay with my reaction to the alien world around
me; I suppose I was always digging in my toes against this
new life to which I had been condemned for the next four
years instead of giving in gracefully to the inevitable. In my
opinion, I considered the first fifteen years of my life had
been, on the whole, reasonably enjoyable; why then change
to the regimented existence of life in a big boarding school? I

felt so ineffectual and incompetent in the midst of so much brain and sophistication, me with my ratty pig-tails, my indoor boots and my stammer.

I found myself to begin with in a form called IVb presided over by a Miss Hughes who also taught history to the whole school. Miss Hughes was very small, dressed in grey, with grey hair and bright blue eyes. She was wonderfully kind to me, taking endless trouble to put me on the right lines in all subjects but try as she would, she could never manage to throw any light on maths. As I struggled up the scholastic ladder I found the mathematical rung always missing and eventually, to my intense relief and I should imagine to the relief of all the good souls who had been struggling with me, I was acknowledged incurably hopeless (number dyslexia perhaps?) and was allowed to switch to the study of harmony and counterpoint instead, which subjects I ultimately passed with distinction in my final exams. I think this deviation from the normal curriculum shows on Miss Mulliner's part a broad and forward-looking attitude for those times which I shall always remember with gratitude.

I am sure this happy solution would never have come about except for the fact that quite soon my musical ability had been recognised and for this distinction I was condemned for three years running to the thrill and terror of playing a solo all alone on the big platform of the Hall packed with parents and their offspring at the yearly Commemoration 'do'. I well remember my first appearance. It should have been my last. Having tottered onto the platform up the little stairs from the 'green room' and receiving all but a mortal blow by the sight of a vast sea of pink expectant faces spread out before me, I managed to get safely to the Bechstein grand and to sit down feeling terribly frightened with not a note of any music, let alone of my 'piece' in my head. On this occasion I had to play a fiendish thing called Rondo Brilliant by Wieniowski which was exactly what it sounded, fast, superficially attractive and ear-catching. But here was the trap; it was so written that if one did not play one or two of the bars leading to the end correctly, one found oneself repeating the thing right from the beginning and could thus go on and on, round and round indefinitely. And this is exactly what I did. At first I did not realise what was happening, being to all intents and purposes only semi-conscious, but after having played the piece through twice it dawned on me that the performance should have been finished some while back. At my third attempt I did manage to find the right way through to bring it to a cascading finish, to my enormous relief. Luckily, nobody except myself and my parents who had heard me practising it time and again at home, was aware of anything amiss. I did not even have a music teacher in the offing liable to a heart attack because I and two other girls shared a first class teacher, a Miss Hirschfeld (Hirstfield, she became during the War) who came down from London to Sherborne every week to give us special tuition.

Besides music, which I think was well taught and which I enjoyed, I became quite good at games and eventually managed to get myself into all the House teams and gym squad and for one fine summer was wicket-keeper in the School first XI (I think the proper one was ill or something). I must confess to some super moments of pride when we, as members of the team due to play a match that Saturday were allowed to descend to breakfast already dressed for the part in our green games skirts (surprisingly mini) which bore the coloured braid of our House just above the hem line. How splendid one felt walking onto the platform and into one's choir seat in this conspicuous rig-out in full view of the whole school gathered for morning prayers! But the wind was very quickly taken out of our sails (or should it be skirts?) as soon as Miss Mulliner entered the Hall. She glided in majestically like a barge under full sail, wearing a long black 'vestment' and coloured stole, followed by the Head of the School carrying an armful of books.

Although I never saw as much of Miss Mulliner as others who were in her House (Aldhelmstead Senior) or who were taught by her (this privilege I did not enjoy till I reached the two top forms) her personality dominated everything; in fact, Miss Mulliner *was* the school.

Humbly we all stood and humbly bowed submissive heads as the great Ship of State sailed slowly past us to her anchorage upon the platform. Miss Mulliner was a large woman, tall, with thin, sandy hair strained back off her face into a small bun. Her large, prominent eyes wandered benignedly over our submissive forms. Those eyes missed absolutely nothing.

As she passed up the aisle the luckier girls on the outside of the lines could catch a glimpse of a pair of large black boots moving stealthily backwards and forwards beneath her robe which was short enough to reveal to their delighted eyes those objects of interest. We did not know why she wore boots; perhaps she had weak ankles like I had. Anyway, they gave her giggling audience something to giggle about. But beneath this outward appearance of a real school-marm, a dragon and a figure of fun, we all knew in our heart of hearts that Miss Mulliner was a wonderful woman personifying every high aspiration that now and then transformed our own hooligan selves into pale images of her splendid one. So while we giggled with amusement, we giggled with respect; while we grumbled and rebelled against her tyrannies we conformed to them because of this respect; she sat so high and firmly on her pedestal that we accepted her without question as the supreme model to which we must aspire.

On re-reading these lines, it strikes me that so far they have given the impression that my school life was passed in joyous sunshine, which is far from the truth because I was always very conscious of the darker side of the cloud, of the small unimportant things in the everyday programme. And these oppressed me unduly. Those long antiseptic school passages smelling repulsively of rubber, leaking gas and coal-tar soap — how I hated them. We would drift along them like ghosts because talking and running were forbidden. Our footfall was reduced to mouse-like scufflings because of rubber on our footwear. Occasionally somebody, late for a lesson might risk a long silent rush to a class room only to be caught in the act by one of the staff or, worse still, by Miss Mulliner herself, popping out of some door. The rest of us, the 'goodies' would smugly continue our dutiful ambling leaving the poor unfortunate victim to her fate. (This was probably nothing worse than a sorrowful ticking off by Miss Mulliner which had a more crushing effect than all the 'lines' devised by the other teachers.)

Another haunting memory is prep. on winter evenings beneath flickering, leaking gas-light. I suppose one was considered lucky to have a desk beneath a light at all, but even so it was a bad light to study by and the whole atmosphere was depressing. One's feet too were always cold, even in boots. Cold feet again undressing for bed in our tiny, chilly cubicles with just enough room for a hard, black bed, small dressing-table-chest-of-drawers, and a wash-stand. In the mornings, we would find the water frozen in our jugs. No hot-water bottles allowed, of course, we had to be spartan. But however much I aspired to be spartan I could never get to sleep in that hostile bed with too few blankets and cold feet. In despair, and I suppose unhygienically, I would wrap my still warm combinations round my icy extremities and found in them some consolation.

And what about Sunday Evensong? Of all the many inducements to bouts of tearful nostalgia the Sunday evening service headed the list. Dressed in our best (what ever for?) we filed into the Hall or to our choir stalls on the platform; the organ swelled and rumbled (or occasionally, when the human blower failed to get the bellows going in time, wailed and expired) Miss Mulliner sailed in and the service began. Another week was about to start and home and everything lovely seemed a terribly long way away. Hymn 477 A. & M.

'The day Thou gavest Lord is ended' etc. or Hymn 20 A. & M. 'At even ere the sun had set' etc. It wasn't only those soul-searing words, but their alliance with those heart-rending tunes which reduced many of us to a sentimental mass of nostalgic yearning.

I suppose in many instances we young things were under considerable strain and anxiety for fathers or brothers involved in the War. I myself, had my dear uncle Maurice to worry about. I remember many instances of the death of someone's father or brother and how pityingly but cruelly we would focus our curiosity on our poor friend to see how she was reacting to the blow. Apart from this, I don't remember being very worried by the war news, until perhaps my last two years. Quite rightly, I think, our normal programme was carried through as usual and school life was to us of more interest and importance than events in Europe. We did have one excitement at least which jolted us out of the normal. Our German mistress who lodged in the town was a Fraulein von Bissing, sister of the notorious and hated General von Bissing who had been one of the commanders in the German invasion of Belgium and had been responsible for many acts of cruelty against the civilian population. One night stones were thrown at her windows by the indignant and enraged townsfolk and for her own safety Fraulein von Bissing was hastily removed and I suppose interned. Our German lessons forthwith ceased and never more materialised.

That December Julian left Eton and passed into Sandhurst; he was not yet eighteen. From that time onwards he was entirely swallowed up by the Army. He had a commission in the Royal Warwickshire Regiment and eventually was based in the Isle of Wight from whence he took drafts of men across the Channel to Boulogne or le Havre while waiting his turn to take the place of one of the many hundreds of boys like himself who had never returned. 'But the War will be over in six months at most,' we said, comforting ourselves. 'It can't possibly last any longer'. But it was still going on and with gathering momentum in December 1915, and the casualty lists in the daily papers grew even longer.

Julian, as busy as ever had yet found time to send me for Christmas the promised Kipling book called *The Days' Work*. It was a slim, red leather-bound volume and on the fly-leaf he had written 'To V.C. from Julian, Christmas 1915', and with two ticks beside the story called 'The Brushwood Boy' which he wanted me to read. He often jokingly called me V.C. and we both would laugh at the very idea. When he was just nineteen, Julian was sent to the Front, onto the Somme, into 'the worst part of the worst battle that ever was fought on all that awful front line' (here I am quoting from a letter written by his mother, Norah Gribble). After six months in the thick of it, Julian collapsed with bad trench fever and eventually arrived home on sick leave. To my fury and indignation at still being a silly useless schoolgirl at Sherborne, I did not see him but before going back to the front again he sent me a badge of the Royal Warwickshires, a button from his tunic and his photograph. He was now a temporary captain in the 10th Battalion.

In spite of the growing anxiety in my mind as in the minds of so many others, the routine of school life had to be tackled with as much vigour and single-minded concentration as though our efforts might, in some miraculous way help to stop the frightful slaughter the other side of the Channel. It was a distraction at least for me to have the training of the House choir for the singing competition to fill my mind and help to blur the thought of Julian in the mud-filled trenches of Flanders.

First I had to choose the people I thought would make a choir. There were some very nice voices in the House, but one or two very good voices do not necessarily make a choir, they must 'blend' properly. So at the risk of mortally offending one or two super warblers who were sure they would be picked, I at last assembled my 'chosen' people.

Stupidly, I cannot remember the name of the 'big wig'

who came from London to judge the competition, more stupidly still, the songs we had to sing. But the result was most gratifying; Dun Holme won.

I was given this job the next year, too, but alas, we lost, by one mark. This was (and I never can quite agree with the reasoning) because, in the adjudicator's opinion we should have sung those songs in the reverse order. As I cannot remember what the songs were, I can't say in which order we sang them, but I *think* we sang the easier one first and the more classical one last which according to the judge was just not done. I was disappointed and felt very contrite at having made the wrong decision and so lost the cup. But our reputation as a choir was, if anything, enhanced by this bit of 'bad luck' as my error of judgement was kindly called.

Some time in 1917, Julian came home on another sick leave and when he was better father and I spent some days visiting his family at Kingston Russell, their lovely home on the Dorset coast. To my intense relief I had only one more term at Sherborne, in my opinion at least one term too long. For the last year I had been chafing against the bit, for were not scores of other girls of my age and even younger already doing something to help in the War effort? I felt deeply ashamed at still being only a school-girl and in a quite unasked-for 'cushy' billet while so many young lives were being thrown away in the shambles of Flanders.

Julian spent that Christmas and his twenty-first birthday in the New Year in the trenches. In spite of this appalling existence he managed to send us all his regimental Christmas card.

At long last, and with no backward glances, I said goodbye to my *Alma Mater* and left, filled with eagerness at the prospect of being able to do something to help finish the War.

16

War Work

━━━

For a long while none of my efforts to be something or do something in the War effort met with any success. Everything I suggested, like joining up in one or other of the Forces or going into a hospital was frowned upon. My parents insisted I stayed at home, the very idea of me stepping out into the world on my own was unthinkable to them. I suppose with their Victorian background and outlook it must have been difficult for them to realise that here was a new world come to stay and not at all a nice one at that. They still clung to the comforting thought that our lives would return to normal after the War, at any rate those of our generation who had survived and that for me and for all young females of our class, life would follow the accepted pattern; we would ultimately have a coming out dance and we would, if we were lucky, because nearly half a million potential husbands of our own age had already been wiped out, marry and raise a family.

Mother spent much of the War at Studland with Rachel who was doing a sort of rest cure because one shoulder had grown higher than the other due to violin playing. (Having some knowledge of the art of violin playing, I can only surmise that her instructress must have been rather an indifferent one.) Anyhow, she stopped learning the violin and concentrated on the usual lessons and keeping goats. My brother was at his prep. school near-by. This simple life kept mother happy and busy. There was no need for her to worry about me, now kicking my heels desperately at home since old family friends, May Campbell and her daughter, Audrey, were now living at Copseham keeping house for my father and me. Very often, Jack, her son spent his leave with us recovering from the all too frequent bouts of trench fever to which he fell victim. Not surprisingly, knowing his character, he had immediately enlisted in the London Scottish at the beginning of the War without waiting for a commission and much to his mother's annoyance. Thus, he could proudly claim to be one of the First Hundred Thousand. He looked splendid in full war paint swinging along in his kilt. In the early war days it did not seem at all strange for the Highland regiments to enter battle in kilts. I can well remember the scene when on one of Jack's leaves his mother found lice crawling between the pleats. Later on this fancy dress was discarded for something less romantic but more practical for trench warfare. Eventually he got a commission in the Black Watch. Apart from the trench fever, Jack went through the whole war otherwise untouched, physically at any rate.

We shared a love of music; in fact Jack's knowledge of it far exceeded mine and in particular the scores of operettas, most of which he knew by heart, as also the casts and dates of production. Many an hour of his leave I spent playing through these operettas to him till I felt ready to drop from the piano stool, completely exhausted. Being able to read musical scores easily can have drawbacks! Jack became one of my trustees and always remained one of my greatest friends. Audrey found work in an aircraft factory near-by but no, this was not for me. At last, after weeks of much rebellious haggling and argument and frustration, May Campbell offered to take me with her to work with a party of Red Cross workers two or three times a week at Ockham Park, Lady Lovelace's beautiful home in Ripley. I have only a vague picture in my mind's eye of a long room overlooking parkland full of mighty cedars with table upon table of hospital equipment over which bent white clad forms with red-crossed bosoms and white swathed heads. There, the very old and the very young alike spent hours rolling bandages and plucking at cotton-wool pads. I, not being really in either category felt that my capabilities were under-estimated. Admittedly I was at last doing something to help, albeit a sad necessity, but I longed for something more glamorous and exciting.

I then heard that help was needed in the canteen at the aeroplane factory where Audrey Campbell was working, so on those days when I was not rolling bandages. I travelled back and forth by train to a small place called Effingham Junction which had suddenly found itself surprisingly important and bursting all over with activity. There I worked, surrounded by huge gas ovens beneath a corrugated iron roof endlessly feeding the tired and sweating shifts as they came from the workshops. This was such arduous, exhausting work that although it could hardly be called glamorous I felt it could be regarded as essential to the prosecution of the War. So I stuck to it for some months till I fell ill with bad tonsilitis. My tonsils had always plagued me from time to time. Authority then commanded that they should be removed and I was put into a nursing home in London. My surgeon, when not engaged in pulling out people's tonsils was apparently a person of some importance as I realised when, having shorn his operating outfit he appeared in full colonel's uniform with miles of ribbons across his chest. Unfortunately, he forbad my return to the ovens and told me to get outdoor work. So I decided to become a land girl.

Every farm by then was short of man labour, in fact no males were to be found on any except the harassed owner and possibly one or two tottering old bodies, conscientious objectors and strange misfits of no use for military service nor for anything else really. Therefore, tough female workers were much in demand and the Women's Land Army became a splendid body of women drawn from all classes of society.

Almost directly opposite Copseham lay Mr. Almond's

Farm. Not a big one, I forget the acreage, but it carried a dairy herd, pigs and poultry, lots of arable land and roots which in those days were extensively fed to the cattle. Mrs. Almond ran the dairy and poultry. We had always bought our milk and butter from this farm and Mr. Almond was woefully short-handed, so I went to him one day and offered my services. He accepted them with not a flicker of a smile upon his long, sad face. His face was very much the shape of an almond, a permanently disillusioned and disapproving almond. It became one of my daily ambitions to make Mr. Almond smile, but I can't remember if I ever did. I then went and got my land girl's outfit, khaki breeches, coat, boots and gaiters and hat, and I was ready to tackle anything that came my way.

But before I could begin playing my new rôle, Europe once again exploded in the long expected spring offensive launched by the Germans and on 23rd March Julian's name was among those reported missing in those long, sad columns in the daily papers. For some time nothing more was heard; then suddenly, wonderful news. Julian had been recommended for the V.C. 'for most conspicuous bravery and devotion to duty'. But his family had still not heard whether he was alive or dead till some while later when they were told that he had been wounded in the battle on Beaumetz-Harmies Ridge in which he had won his V.C. and had been taken as prisoner to Germany. Very slowly and irregularly more news began trickling in. Julian himself wrote to his mother a month or so later saying his head wound had healed and that he was soon to be transferred to a military fortress prison at Mainz on the Rhine. It was not till July that he heard the news of his V.C. award in a letter from his mother. In reply he says with characteristic modesty, 'I must say it was a terrific surprise but, of course, they are not as uncommon as they used to be'. And to his sister, Barbara, he writes, 'I should not be at all surprised if the V. is not a misprint for M. but anyhow the cat is out of the bag as it was on the envelope and I have been carried round the camp in a most uncomfortable and embarrassing position.'

Now it was my turn to flounder in mud-filled fields, though only of Mr. Almond's Farm and this I did with a lighter heart now I knew that Julian, though wounded and a prisoner was out of the 'hot war'. 'And surely,' we said, 'it couldn't be *so* long now before the end?'

Every morning at six I trundled across to the farm to help with the milking. I confess I have forgotten how many cows had to be milked — by hand of course. I know that the four of us, Mr. Almond, Willum, the ancient farm hand, Daisy and I were at it for what seemed a very long time. What would I have done without Daisy? I can't remember her other name. She was an erstwhile London housemaid, now a jolly, plump milkmaid with a laugh and a joke for everything funny and not so funny. She was a grand person to work with, making light of many of the less attractive sides of farm work and many a giggle we shared over the tedious and unglamorous chores. She relished, as I did, the picture we made toiling together — she, the once prim London housemaid in dainty pink frock, starched cap and apron and I, the budding debutante ear-marked for a coming out dance at the Ritz when the War was over, cleaning out the pig-styes and the cow-stalls, turning the butter-churn endlessly and struggling with bad mannered cows. How our wrists and hands ached with the unaccustomed pulling and squeezing! Twice a day, too. It was nice though to bury one's head in the warm, milk-smelling flank of one's bovine victims, while beseeching them to remain calm and to let down their milk. Mr. Almond, when he had finished his lot of cows (he worked much, much faster than we did) would come and stand behind us — his long, sad face even longer and sadder as he watched our fumbling fingers struggling with recalcitrant teats. And, of course, everything always went wrong when he was there; the cows would suddenly swish their dungy tails across our faces or plunge a foot into the pail of milk sending it flying across the floor. No, Mr. Almond was *never* amused.

Good old Daisy, I wonder what became of her? I remember her once saying that nothing would drag her back again into service, farming was the life for her. I know that when I had given in my notice and left, soon after the War had ended, and plunged into round upon round of hectic gaiety, Daisy stayed on, for how long I do not know. The men would soon be getting demobilised and returning to civvy street, wanting jobs. Would Daisy have to step aside for one of them I wondered? How Mr. Almond would miss her. She was the backbone of the farm, capable of running the whole show. The only thing she could not do as well as I, was drive the horse; she had never had the chance to learn. So I was one up on her and was sent out every day, wet or fine, with the horse and the milk float and the big brass milk can by my side, to deliver milk to all the houses in the area. From years of practice, the horse knew exactly where to stop to allow me to fill the jugs and trip up to the back doors. Coming back milkless, but full of cash, we rattled home along the road in fine style. I felt like a Roman charioteer standing on my platform, tickling old Bess up with my whip so that occasionally she broke into a clattering canter. Old Willum would scratch his disapproving head as Bess and I swept into the yard with everything jingling and shaking. But it was good fun. Less good fun was the arduous task of taking the enormous old cart horse and cart across the fields to dig and load up turnips and mangolds. These we had to put through the cutting machine, a seemingly never-ending and exhausting job.

Now and then I managed to 'get off' to go with father to some sort of social do in London, a concert in the dear old Queen's Hall, an exhibition and reception at his club, the Burlington Fine Arts. And once, and this was the first time ever, I went to a ball. Because it was the first dance I had been to, bar one or two small private affairs and as it was war-time, I can remember the occasion well and the reason for it. Throughout the War, there had always been a certain amount of entertaining going on for the Dominion fighting forces passing through London on their way to the Front or spending their leave there. Two of these energetic organising hostesses were Lady Harrowby and her daughter, Lady Frances Ryder, their headquarters being their London house, 19 Grosvenor Place. It was through them somehow or other that I was included in a party going to one of these dances, not in London, but if I remember rightly at Grantham. I know it entailed a long train journey and I think I must have stayed with Sir Alfred and Lady Welby, great friends of my parents. Of course my maid travelled with me; it would have been unthinkable for me to go by myself and she was indeed most useful in getting me unpacked, my dress ironed out and myself eventually arrayed in all my glory.

Somehow my hosts must have spread the news that this was my first big dance so that to my surprise and no little alarm, I beheld a posse of eager, khaki-clad young men gathered round the foot of the staircase down which I was descending. I was all in white with a blue ribbon in my hair. What a thrill at being the centre of attraction and of having so many young men all clamouring for a dance. I was kept hard at it filling up the programme dangling from my wrist on its white cord. I never stopped dancing the whole evening and found all my partners charming. There were four whom I especially liked, a Canadian, an Australian, a New Zealander and a South African, but by the end of the evening it was the Canadian I had fallen for. Captain Shore was a young padré on his way to the front. He was a splendid looking fellow, tall with fresh complexion and bright blue eyes. His hair was grey which, strangely, made him look absurdly young. On our way back to London next day he read poetry to me in the train while my maid and his three Dominion friends sat opposite us looking rather embarrassed, poor things! I can remember being very cautious about this adventure when the family began probing. Somehow I felt that had I disclosed my feelings about Captain Shore that, for one thing I would not have been believed, and for another a Canadian Padré could not possibly have been taken seriously. He certainly didn't seem to fit into the Doughty House entourage, but to me he seemed like a breath of fresh air and I didn't think much of myself for being too cowardly to introduce him to the family. We wrote to each other and when he was lying wounded in a London hospital some months later, I went twice to see him. In spite of this romance I am not sure what his christian name was — I remember it began with an *H* — I always thought of him as Captain Shore and I suppose he must have been a Reverend, too. I am almost certain he eventually married a school friend of mine.

After this Cinderella-like adventure I returned to the mud and the cows and no further interruptions, at any rate of such magnitude, disturbed my rather common task and daily round.

17

Armistice

———◆———

We never, ever had any doubts that the Allies were going to win the War; the question was, when? The Germans had launched their all-out spring offensive under the leadership of their brilliant General Ludendorf before the Americans arrived 'en masse' so that until the tide turned against the enemy in the late summer, the Allies were really fighting 'with their backs to the wall'. From the dim memories of those far-off days, the names of Douglas Haig and Ludendorf stand out clearly. A foolish memory attaches itself to both those names.

After the Armistice I found time, amid my riotous sportings in the mad aftermath of post-war reaction, to do something less enjoyable but more *pro bono publico*. This was working twice a week in a crêche in the Notting Hill area, nearly as insalubrious then as it is now. The crêche was run for the benefit of babies whose mothers were working most of the day for one reason or another, and as I and others like myself, were not working at all, we could hardly turn a deaf ear when the cries for help went out. The mums would arrive and thrust into our unwilling arms their offspring with instructions on how to feed little so and so, together with a bottle of milk and, with any luck one dry nappy. Thus equipped for a morning or afternoon's work, we set to. For my sins I was detailed to look after one of the most pathetic of the little odoriferous bundles of misery; its name was Douglas Haig King, aged three months. I couldn't begin to count the miles I must have covered walking up and down that room with Douglas Haig King cradled in my arms trying to soothe him into slumber, if only for a few minutes.

As for Ludendorf, whose brilliant strategy nearly brought disaster to the allied armies in the spring of 1918, his name for a while glowed with the red glare of destruction. Like Napoleon in his all-conquering triumphs, Ludendorf was the bogey-man of those last war months, though I never remember hearing that bad little children were scared into becoming good little children as in Boney's days with the threat that 'Ludendorf will get you if you don't behave yourself'. All the more surprising to remember that we dubbed a friend of ours whose name was Lyonulph Tolle-mache, then a house-master at Bradfield College, 'Luden-dorf'. Whether this was because we imagined we saw signs of teutonic discipline and drive bursting out of him (he certainly roared at the boys) or because both names were long and both began with an L. I fancy a little of both. Anyhow poor Lyonulph was Ludendorf for many a year.

To return to that agonising spring and summer. Even I, off the map as it were, labouring safely in the quiet fields of a country farm was very much aware of the tension of the long drawn out struggle in France. The monotony of my work was broken for me from time to time by London outings of one kind or another and always when Jack Campbell came back on leave. Then, if he was not on sick leave we would go to London to see a play or one of his adored 'musicals'. *Chu Chin Chow* was one of them. It enjoyed a phenomenal run at 'His Majesty's' with Oscar Asche and Lily Brayton the stars. I saw it at least five times, if not more, with various young khaki-clad friends home on leave. Then came the influenza epidemic which began in the East and spread throughout the world, arriving in England in the autumn. Whether the type of influenza was an unusually virulent sort or brought death to so many victims because of war exhaustion has never been proved. What is certain is that this world plague added immensely to the strain of that year. We, as a family luckily escaped. In a post-card from Julian from his fortress prison on the Rhine he says he 'hopes we are all right and have escaped this awful plague from Spain'. I cannot remember getting any letters from him, only post-cards. He was restricted to two letters and four post-cards a month. I wrote now and again but I think many letters, not surprisingly, went astray. In one of his bi-monthly letters to his mother he says, 'I have now had forty-eight letters and two post-cards since I have been prisoner (just over five months, which doesn't sound many)'.

The end of the War came quickly at the end of the autumn. It was precipitated by the flood of American troops by then pouring into France and by the Allied blockade which was relentlessly wearing down the enemy's morale. I can recall the excitement when the Kaiser fled to Holland and a few days later abdicated. All this and mutinies in all branches of the German services heralded the inevitable ending and on 11th November the Armistice was signed.

Try as I will, I simply cannot remember anything to mark that day for me as being any different from any other. We had no little transistor sets to babble out news as we worked and no radio to listen to at home when the day's work was finished. London and all towns and villages went mad, of course; we in our quiet country surroundings had no celebrations. When I did at last hear the news which must have been that same day sometime, my first feeling was of complete thankfulness that the guns had stopped their massacre and that there would be no more killings and that Julian and all prisoners of war would soon be free and on their way home.

But this was not to be, for Julian. On 25th November, two weeks after the armistice had been signed and on the day many of his fellow prisoners were leaving for home, Julian died of double pneumonia after influenza. He is buried in the cemetery at Mainz.

3710